This second edition is dedicated to the memory of Phyl who, still a student at the age of 88, read a university course text on the state of society today and said:

'I think I know what the answer is - it's all to do with information ...'

The Essence of
Information Systems

The Essence of Management Series

The Essence of Information Systems

Second Edition

CHRIS EDWARDS, JOHN WARD
AND ANDY BYTHEWAY

Prentice Hall

London   New York   Toronto   Sydney   Tokyo   Singapore
Madrid   Mexico City   Munich

2005

First published 1991
This second edition first published 1995 by
Prentice Hall International (UK) Limited
Campus 400, Maylands Avenue
Hemel Hempstead
Hertfordshire, HP2 7EZ
A division of
Simon & Schuster International Group

© Prentice Hall International (UK) Ltd, 1991, 1995

Printed and bound in Great Britain by
T J Press, Padstow, Cornwall

Library of Congress Cataloging-in-Publication Data

Available from the publisher

British Library Cataloguing in Publication Data

A catalogue record for this book is available from
the British Library

ISBN 0-13-359308-8

---

2 3 4 5   99 98 97 96

Contents

Contents

Preface

Since the first edition of this book the general level of interest in information systems and their contribution to business has continued to increase; this book deals with the subject from a *management* and *business* perspective. It focuses on the way in which business strategy is served by information systems, and explains the tools and techniques that will help to ensure that information systems strategies are in line with strategic business needs. In this second edition there is new material on business process redesign, process and information analysis, requirements analysis, outsourcing and trends.

Information systems management is still a young subject, and there are no ground rules that provide an easy, prescriptive understanding of what 'best practice' might be. Technology continues to change rapidly, undermining the ability of technical people to develop a reliable and manageable approach to their work. It also prevents the development of a stable relationship with the IT supply industry. Within the business itself, information systems users continue to develop their level of competency and understanding, and therefore their level of expectation and their ability to articulate needs.

In this situation the only sensible approach is to step back from the particular (which changes from year to year, and even from week to week) and to try and understand the underlying principles which will provide a more enduring understanding of successful information systems management. This is the general approach taken in this book. In it there are no detailed descriptions of 'methodologies', nor of current products and services. Instead we prefer to use some traditional and some new management ideas, to understand the benefits that information systems can provide and the means to achieve them, whatever the particular circumstances might be. We hope that this book will be interesting to a wide audience, especially practising business managers, students of business administration, and

IT product and service suppliers who wish to understand more about the managerial perspective on information systems.

Our thanks are due to many who have made this book possible. Especially to Dawn, Christine, Lisa, Jackie and Pam, who helped with production in different ways, and 'kept shop' while we were totally occupied with the book's content. Also, to all those MBA students and practising managers who have helped us to shape our ideas over the last few years.

Chris Edwards
John Ward
Andy Bytheway
Cranfield School of Management, June 1995

1

Setting the scene

For some thirty years organizations have been developing computer-based information systems. Before this people, paper, pens, calculators and mechanical punch card machines were the main tools available for data manipulation. These tools and even the early computers were awkward to use and much effort was expended in ensuring they were used efficiently and correctly. However, over the last thirty years the technology has been developing very quickly and hence new problems associated with its use have tended to appear with alarming frequency. It was fruitless to focus upon the potential offered by this developing technology until the technical problems of its operation were more or less stabilized. The tasks undertaken by the early computer equipment were those which were the most obvious to identify and the easiest for the computer to improve, such as accounting, invoicing, and other labour intensive data-based office activities of the 1950s and 1960s. This is not meant as a criticism of the early developers of information systems - it would have been disastrous to apply the early computer technology to anything more sophisticated until it was better understood and proven.

A framework for understanding

The structure of this book is based on the separation of certain ideas:

- first, *supply* and *demand* as different viewpoints on the provision of business information systems;

- second, *strategy* and *tactics* as different levels of thinking associated with different timescales.

IS and IT: supply and demand

The vast majority of the issues addressed throughout the 1960s, 1970s and even the early 1980s were issues associated with how to 'supply' information systems to business. As the supply issues have become better understood, and with many of the basic systems of organizations having been automated, attention has turned to more imaginative and fruitful applications of the technology.

This shift of attention has highlighted new issues associated with ascertaining 'demand' for information systems in organizations. No longer are organizations content to focus upon the obvious - they are now searching for new opportunities. The mid-1980s saw the development of several techniques to help analyze an organization's objectives and methods of operation in order to reveal more innovative opportunities based on information systems. This focus on ascertaining demand has not detracted from issues of supply, but rather has broadened the range of matters to be considered. The focus of the late 1980s was upon the importance of determining demand, often driven by the need to use information systems to gain competitive advantage for business, or at least to avoid being disadvantaged.

Supply issues are very much the province of information technology managers and specialists - often the people who have developed with the technology during the 1960s and 1970s. In this book supply issues will be referred to as information technology (IT) issues.

Compare the typical IT person with those that are able to analyze the business using an intimate knowledge of the business process to reveal opportunities. Usually such knowledge is accumulated by management and functional specialists and can be applied by them in deciding what the organization needs in terms of information systems. Ascertaining demand is a management task and the issues concerned will be referred to in this book as information systems (IS) issues.

The phrases IS and IT cannot be assumed to have exclusive and distinctive definitions because some of the issues associated with matching supply and demand overlap. However, some distinction needs to be made between supply and demand issues - Figure 1.1 summarizes the differences.

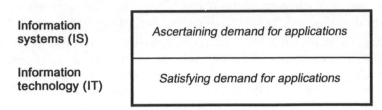

| Information systems (IS) | Ascertaining demand for applications |
| Information technology (IT) | Satisfying demand for applications |

Figure 1.1   The prime issues

Strategy and tactics

Both IS and IT have 'strategic' and 'tactical' components. By strategic we mean those issues of a longer term nature which require to be addressed by senior management relatively infrequently. By tactical we mean those issues of an operational short-term nature which are generally the concern of middle management and specialists. Strategy involves creating a vision of the future and the means and policies which will enable the organization to reach that vision, whereas tactical matters are concerned with applying the rules and creating applications. Clearly these descriptions are very general and more precise definitions will be presented as the book progresses.

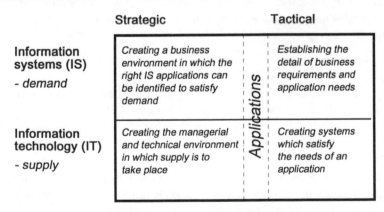

Figure 1.2   Management issues

Figure 1.2 relates the strategic and tactical notions to the earlier discussion of IS and IT. The contents of the four quadrants show the basic issues of concern to each box. Note that the concept of the 'application' comes between strategic and tactical thinking.

Strategy is concerned with managing *demand*, and optimizing the *benefits* that new applications will provide; tactics are about managing *supply*, and optimizing the *cost* of development and operations. If strategy is managed well but the tactical response is not, nothing will be achieved. If tactics are managed well but strategy is not, then beautiful systems may be delivered, but they will serve no useful business purpose.

Strategic IS

For example, the board members of every large organization need to ensure that the general managers in each business unit consider how applications of information technology can enhance it and underpin its competitive position. This is a strategic IS issue which can be accomplished in a variety of ways, for example by insisting that such matters are dealt with in the business plans submitted to the board members.

Suppose that a key supplier to a large retailer wanted to use EDI (Electronic Data Interchange) as a means of enhancing its relationship with the retailer, and that both parties have agreed to the development of a closer business partnership in all senses: for the managers in charge of buying (in the retailer) and selling (in the supplier) the way in which this is supported by systems is a strategic information systems issue.

Tactical IS

Turning to tactical IS, business unit managers need to ascertain the systems required to operate in their business unit. They must rank their importance to provide priorities for the suppliers of these systems. This can be achieved in a variety of ways by the business, but in practice it is often delegated to consultants.

For the chief buyer in the retailer organization (above), making sure that the detailed application requirements are properly understood is a tactical IS issue, requiring competent and detailed business systems analysis.

Strategic IT

The supply of applications and all of the technology that goes with them can be managed in many ways. For example, it may be possible to supply every person in the organization with a personal computer and to allow every application to be developed separately; an alternative would be a centralized supply strategy based on a central unit and operating on a centrally located machine.

Continuing the retailer-supplier example, EDI services can be acquired from a third party network operator or they can be arranged through private or public networks. This is one aspect of a wider strategic IT matter concerning the use of third party services. It should therefore be dealt by reference to general rules for the use of third party services across all applications.

Tactical IT

The last of the four boxes concerns tactical IT issues. This box embraces all the detailed issues of acquiring and using a particular application.

If a supplier and retailer are to implement EDI, someone needs to evaluate the impact on existing systems and arrange for changes to be made where necessary, and there needs to be a review and specification of the security requirements for data exchange between the two organizations. This is tactical IT.

Levels of management

We must expect different levels of management to become involved with the different areas of concern:

- *strategic IS* is the concern of senior managers, corporate board members and business unit managers;
- *tactical IS* is the province of the managers of particular business units and their operational managers;
- *strategic IT* is an issue to be addressed jointly by senior management/corporate board members and senior IT managers;
- *tactical IT* is an issue to be addressed jointly by IT staff, managers of particular business units and managers working at a functional level within the business unit.

Observation of the real world would suggest that this is not always understood by those concerned and that tasks are often not undertaken by those managers specified. Frequently the IT management is charged with most of these duties but when attempting to discharge them has little success. It is then blamed for systems that do not meet business requirements. Figure 1.3

summarizes the appropriate management to deal with each of the four areas in the general framework.

	Strategic	Tactical
Information systems (IS)	Corporate board members and business unit managers	Business unit managers and functional/operational managers
Information technology (IT)	Corporate board members and senior IT managers	IT staff, business unit managers and functional level management

Figure 1.3   Management concerned

This book considers all four areas, focusing upon the management issues in each box. Technical aspects such as selecting the appropriate programming language for an application (a tactical IT issue) are excluded, as they are not a concern of the intended readership of this book.

The structure and purpose of the book

Chapter 2 is concerned with various ways of classifying IS and IT to demonstrate the breadth of the subject and the types of information system addressed by the book. Chapter 3 raises some of the management issues involved as, historically, the subject has been the province of the technician and without some clarification our focus could cause problems for some readers. Interestingly, many of the problems of the subject are assumed to be technical in origin when in reality they occur because of insufficient or inadequate management activity. The following four chapters (4, 5, 6 and 7) consider the issues of strategic IS, tactical IS, strategic IT and tactical IT respectively. Chapter 8 deals with the support that is needed for successful application development and Chapter 9 discusses organizational issues. Chapter 10 provides some concluding thoughts on current and future directions.

Sequence

This book is not for 'dipping into'. It begins by introducing ideas and a simple vocabulary that is extended as the book progresses. It follows that reading Chapter 8 in isolation would be non-productive - it is necessary to read the preceding chapters first. It would be the delight of the authors to provide definitive answers to all the issues raised but, alas, such answers are not readily available as yet. We are dealing with a very young discipline with a history of scarcely more than thirty years. If the reader is looking for the certainty of the more mature subjects such as accountancy he or she will be disappointed.

Benefits to be gained

The benefits to be gained from studying this book will vary depending upon the focus and organizational level of the reader. However, the benefits outlined below will apply to all the parties involved in the IS/IT process.

- The book will provide an understanding of the framework in which activities of the individual parties should take place. Readers should be able to appreciate where their particular activity is required and also where it is not required: or it could prevent normal managers becoming born-again IT experts!
- Additionally the book will provide an overview of the tools required to ascertain the 'IS demand' for a business and the alternative methods of 'IT supply'.
- Finally, it will assist senior managers in expressing their requirements to more junior staff.

Therefore, we can state very clearly what this book will not do - it will not assist you in understanding the technical issues of computing. For example, if you are not sure of the relative benefits of Ethernet and twisted pair links as means of local area networking at the start, you will still be unsure at the end. Throughout the book we take a *management* perspective.

2

What are information systems?

With a discipline as young as information systems, definitions of what is included and what is excluded are difficult. As a means of portraying boundaries we will describe a day in the life of a marketing executive working for an international games producer.

First the events in the day will be explained and then a number of classifications will be analyzed drawing upon the earlier discussion for examples (see the boxed text below). The description of John's day focuses upon his receipt, despatch and processing of information because this aspect is the focus of this book. However, even if we took a more balanced view of John's day it would still show that information processing is a central feature of the managing in business.

John is awakened at six-thirty a.m. as usual to hear the morning business news - the dollar has fallen yet again. While shaving he wonders how those US sales targets will ever be reached. Still, that problem is for later; first he must fight the crowds on British Rail today he might even get a seat! Arriving at the station John meets Peter York who is the general manager responsible for UK production. After the usual moans about British Rail, John learns of major sourcing difficulties with plastic playing pieces from their Hong Kong subcontractor. John remembers thinking this could happen, but was assured the matter was under control. The new products will probably not be ready for delivery which will not please the customers. No doubt he will be told of the problem formally in due course.

British Rail must be having a good day because he is early to the office and is greeted by Gill, his super-efficient secretary. He notes the morning mail, especially a note from the public relations agency which will require urgent action. He scribbles his comments on the letter and sends it to the chief executive. The telephone book tells him of ten calls still awaiting reply. Possibly more importantly Gill tells him of the dissatisfaction in the sales office with at least five of the clerks talking of looking for new jobs. Still all that can wait a while.

Turning to his newly installed personal computer he logs-on to the electronic mail system to find he has fifteen new messages awaiting reading. He is amazed how this new form of communication has grown over the last two years - nearly everyone in the company is now on the system. He scans the titles of the messages and finds that at least half are copies of reports sent to other people in his department and have been copied to him for his information. This seems to be happening more these days with the new technology. At least the document he really wants is there, which is the periodic international sales report. He reads this very carefully and attempts to draw conclusions from the mass of statistics presented. He notes the compiler has attempted to draw just such conclusions but he always prefers his own interpretation rather than that of others he has not even met. Moving on he notes a request for a meeting from his manager which is hardly a real 'request' but more a summons! He notes this in his pocket diary and tells Gill to put it in the desk diary.

So to the first meeting of the day which is a discussion of the arrangements for a new product launch. John thinks these meetings drag on because the chairman does not control the attendees - John makes a mental note to arrange a showing of the John Cleese video on meetings. However, this is unlikely to happen because his mental notes have a habit of creating little action. Arriving back at the office he telephones a product manager to ask for more information on the item under discussion at the meeting. He is surprised to learn that the product is unlikely to be available on time and hence the whole meeting was rather pointless. However, he will need the information for the following season's launch so he tells the subordinate to produce the analysis anyway.

The detail of the international sales report arrives, this time on paper, so John takes out the vital statistics and prepares a management commentary for the directors which he then gives to Gill to action on her word processor. He tells Gill to telefax it to the director upon completion of the typing.

On leaving the office for lunch he notices Gill dealing with a large pile of documents - she tells him that these are new staff slips, one per employee, being processed for a secretary in an adjoining office who is particularly busy. The lunch is with a long-standing and loyal customer who inadvertently tells John of a major promotion for a new range of products being proposed by a competitor.

more ...

On returning to the office John sends an electronic message to all his product managers reporting this gem of information.

Then it is back to boredom - authorizing salesmen's bonuses. He wonders why he has to do this every month as he seldom changes anything. As a break he enters the information gained at lunch into the competitor database, wondering all the time if he is the only person to update this database. Then, more bonuses to authorize punctuated only by a break to access an external database held by a trade association to which the company belongs. There is no indication at all on this database that the competitor mentioned at lunch is contemplating an expansion of the product range.

For another break he wanders off to see Jim Wallace, a friend who runs the data processing department. Discussions of football and the tribulations of Luton Town lead Jim to explain how busy his department is. Apparently the number of invoices produced in the last week exceeded the previous maximum. John knows that this does not necessarily mean a higher sales volume in the next month's statistics but it is a positive sign. John has a cup of coffee and then returns to his office for the next meeting.

John had been looking forward to this meeting all week because the system under discussion will ease his life considerably. Linking his company's computer with that of his major customers has been in operation for two years, but the new proposal is to extend this to allow customers to see the company's stock levels and vice versa. John will support the matter in any way he can. The meeting ends with a firm timetable for implementation, but John wonders whether the consultancy will deliver the software on time.

John then starts his journey home after another tiring day. He checks the electronic mail on his portable - just more junk mail and copies of other people's letters sent for information. Another day ends as it began with the nine p.m. news reporting that the dollar is down again.

Classification of systems

There are several different ways in which we can classify systems:

- by the degree of formality;
- by the degree or extent of automation applied to them;
- by their relation to decision making;
- by the nature of input and output;
- by the source and degree of tailoring;
- by the value to the organization.

These classifications are discussed in the paragraphs below, using the example of John's day as a means of illustration.

Informal and formal systems

The first classification is based on the difference between informal and formal information systems. The information gleaned on the train, that received from Gill regarding low motivation levels in the sales department and that vital piece of information received at lunch were not the result of a designed process. It could be said that they occurred by accident. For example, nobody designed the fact that Peter York caught the same train as John. Compare this with the international sales report which clearly arrived as a result of a more formal, designed process.

However, the matter may not be as clear as this - it could be that the lunchtime entertaining of the customer was designed for just the outcome described, namely the collection of information. Some organizations try to formalize the informal. The American tradition of the Friday 'beer-bash' - when people stop work early to drink beer and meet other organizational members - is an example of formalizing the informal. The important point is that this book is focusing on designed (formal) information systems and not informal systems. However, sight must never be lost of the existence of the informal and the superb way in which it can operate. Sometimes rumours can spread faster than paperwork and carry the true facts!

Associated with the formal/informal classification is the notion of routine and non-routine information. Routine implies that the information is produced to some timetable, for example the periodic international sales report. Non-routine information is produced as it is required and may not ever be produced again. John's entry of data to the competitor database is an example of a non-routine activity.

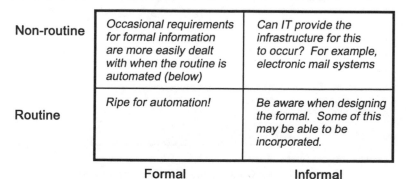

	Formal	Informal
Non-routine	*Occasional requirements for formal information are more easily dealt with when the routine is automated (below)*	*Can IT provide the infrastructure for this to occur? For example, electronic mail systems*
Routine	*Ripe for automation!*	*Be aware when designing the formal. Some of this may be able to be incorporated.*

Figure 2.1   Mapping by formality and routine

Mapping formal/informal with routine/non-routine leads to the arrangement of ideas in Figure 2.1. Routine/formal activity is ripe for automation, whereas the non-routine/informal activity is nearly impossible to plan and hence generic systems like electronic mail are the limit of the activity. Interestingly routine/formal information is usually associated with junior and middle management whereas non-routine/informal is associated with senior management.

Automation

A second important classification is that between manual systems (for example the hand written comments on public relations' letter) and computer-based systems (for example the electronic mail system). This book focuses primarily upon computer-based systems, but the tools of analysis to be presented are valid equally for manual systems, although a little over-complex for such simple systems.

The boundary between the two is less clear as more software is used in what were once entirely manual or electro-mechanical systems. For example, telephone switchboards are now largely computer driven and the data relating to telephone calls become available for further use and analysis. This allows the switchboard - if required - to become an element in a management information system.

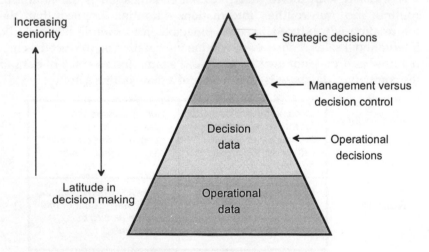

Figure 2.2   Mapping by level of decision making

Relationship with decision making

During John's day he received volumes of information from other organization members which he summarized and passed upwards in the hierarchy. This is a very typical management practice. Figure 2.2 illustrates this process by dividing the decisions made by managements into three types.

Strategic decisions

The first type, often called strategic decisions, relates to those long range, complex and unstructured decisions said to be made by senior management. Information for such decisions is often ill defined, required on a non-recurrent basis, originates from sources external to the organization, gathered in an informal way, and highly summarized. Systems to supply such information to senior management are known as 'executive information systems'. John adding his piece of gossip gained at the lunch table is a way of formalizing what in the past may have been lost information.

Management control decisions

The second type of decisions illustrated in Figure 2.2 are often called management control decisions and are taken by middle managers. These often result from comparing some information to a standard or budget and any difference forces the consideration of alternative courses of action. Information for such decisions is often internally focused, short term, historical, relatively easily predefinable, and required on a routine basis. John was dealing with such information when he examined the periodic international sales report. He could have been looking at the report with certain expectations in mind and he was in fact looking for variations from his expectations.

Operational decisions

The third type of decisions illustrated in Figure 2.2 are termed operational decisions. Here the rules for taking the decision are well understood, to the extent that they can be programmed within a computer system. For example, stock control is a reasonably well understood process and given values for certain variables, such as the cost of keeping a particular item in stock for a certain length of time, a computer can perform a set of predefined steps and make the decision. It becomes a matter of choice whether management or the computer takes a decision, but this does not change the fact that the decision is an operational one. Information for such decisions is well understood, internally focused, predefinable and precise. Given that such decisions are made frequently (possibly many thousands of times per day within an organization) it would appear sensible to consider the use of a computer. John's task of authorizing salesmen's bonuses is an example of the use of this kind of information.

In addition to all of this information required for making decisions, a need exists to generate and manage the operating data of the business: for example, accounting data, payroll data, order processing and invoicing data. These data are not required for decision making but must exist for the business to continue operating. Such data can be predefined, tend not to change very much through time and need to be very precise. The automatic production of invoices would be an example of such data. Notice how data at this level are not produced for management purposes but will comprise the basis of management information when analyzed at a later point in time. Management would therefore only become concerned if the data were *not* produced.

Input and output

A fourth important classification of the systems is that all of the systems mentioned in John's day consisted of an input element, a process element and an output element - the process element may have some aspect of storage contained within it (see Figure 2.3). The value to its user of any particular system will arise from one or a number of these elements being automated or otherwise supported by an automated system.

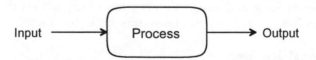

Input ⟶ Process ⟶ Output

Figure 2.3 Input, process and output

For example, the electronic mail system used by John will have:

- an input element (functions to assist with the composition of the message);
- a processing element (message storage and movement); and

14

- an output function (which allows the recipient to collect, read and store the message, as required).

In these activities John was directly involved in the input and output processes.

Compare this system with the invoicing system, in which:

- input would probably be undertaken by data entry clerks at visual displays;

- processing would consist of selecting the appropriate price from a price database and possibly a product description, calculating the total cost of the many items on the invoice, and calculating sales or value added tax;

- output may well consist of presenting the results of processing in the form of an invoice. Alternatively output from the system may be over telephone lines linked direct to the purchaser's computer.

Again, all the elements exist but the value of processing is considerably greater than in the first example. It can be seen that John is sometimes part of the input process and sometimes part of the output process.

All of the systems John used consisted of a number of components: some of these were technical, for example his new personal computer, and some were human, for example Gill was a component in the word processing system, used for the production of the report to John's manager. Some of the systems were sophisticated, again for example the personal computer, and some were not, for example the pencil used to write on the letter from the public relations company. Some of the components would be seen traditionally as belonging to the discipline of data processing, namely the computers and the digital communication aspects, whereas others would not, for example the telephone and the telefax equipment. However, all of these aspects are part of information systems as defined in this book.

Source and degree of tailoring

A fifth classification of information systems could consist of the source and degree of tailoring of the system. Some systems are produced especially for a single organization. John's competitor database was probably at least tailored for his organization to reflect the information it was wished to store. However, other systems, for example the electronic mail system, may be identical in John's organization to that used in many others, no tailoring of the system being necessary to satisfy the organizational needs.

Value to the organization

The sixth and final classification of information systems to be discussed here focuses upon the way in which the system provides value to the organization. Additionally, it represents the evolution of data processing in many organizations, which is also illustrated in Figure 2.4. This figure also provides an overview of the evolution of systems over the past thirty or so years, and shows how thinking has migrated from systems providing purely internal (and relatively limited) benefits to much more ambitious systems which stretch beyond the boundaries of one organization, and may involve whole industries.

A model of the evolution of systems

Using the evolutionary model in Figure 2.4 we can trace the way in which the application of information systems (and the benefits obtained) have developed over seven stages.

	Efficiency	Effectiveness	Business integration
Internal focus	1 *Traditional data processing (accounting, payroll)*	2 *Core operational systems (online, real time, MIS)*	3 *Internal integration (end-to-end links)*
External focus	4 *Electronic data interchange (direct ordering, invoices)*	5 *Rationalization of processes Sharing of information (stock levels, price files)*	6 *External integration (Supply chain optimization)*

Accepts current business form ⟶ Changes business form ⟶

Figure 2.4   The evolution of information systems

Stage 1: Internal efficiency

Initial activity in most organizations (typically about 30 years ago for the 'early adopters') concentrated on developing systems for the purpose of improving internal efficiency. Tasks that were already undertaken by clerks were computerized and in essence efficiency meant an intention to reduce staffing levels. Tasks such as invoicing, accounting and order processing were developed to mimic the manual activities replaced. The data processing department had been born.

Information technology tools were developed to meet the needs of such systems. As explained in Chapter 1, the problems were mostly technical and large numbers of technicians were recruited. Systems flexibility was not especially important as the systems developed did not change very much through time. In the case above, the invoices produced in the data processing department would be an example of such information.

Stage 2: Internal effectiveness

As time passed attention turned towards using the vast quantities of information stored in the computer for the purpose of management information. This type of information related to the internal workings of the organization, and thus the phrase 'management information systems' had been originated. Major problems developed because the tools available to develop systems were those first used for data processing. Flexibility was required by the users who wished to amend the system as their needs changed; however, the systems were inflexible and difficult to change.

The answer to this problem was provided later by the personal computer and it became the fashion to supply a manager with a microcomputer. Support would be provided for technical needs, but typically all development of the system was left to the manager. This tended to lead to fragmentation and duplication in systems. Sharing data between departments slowed the development of the system and hence each department tended to develop systems independently - yet using similar data.

Additionally, some of the issues solved by the data processing professionals in the first stage tended to surface again, for example documentation of personally developed systems can be a little inadequate. However, even considering these problems many hundreds of systems were developed by some organizations. In the case above, the periodic international sales report would be an example of this type of information usage. [1]

---

[1]   Note that these first two stages endorsed the existing form of the business and did not make any significant changes to its form or structure. This two stage pattern progressed into the early 1980s when a new era emerged with the idea of using

Stage 3: Internal integration

Moving to Stage 3 involved attempting to integrate by way of sharing data or systems between the various functions of the business. As an example, imagine a motor car manufacturer which decided to provide a very high degree of personalization on each car yet to maintain manufacturing costs within the mass produced sector of the market. The personalization would extend to choice of internal trim colour, a choice from six sets of wheels, four sun-roofs, etc. Altogether there would be some sixty 'options'. The cars would be truly 'bespoke' at little more than the cost of a mass produced car. Added to this a high level of customer service in every aspect would be vital as the cars were to appeal to the discerning customers.

The information system to support this would allow a detailed specification of the car to be produced in the showroom on a visual display unit connected to the manufacturer's computer. After specification the computer would try to locate such a car at other dealers, or attempt to locate one in the delivery system. If this was unsuccessful it would then schedule the car onto the assembly line if all the components were available, otherwise it would electronically chase missing components from the supplier and then schedule manufacture. When the system has decided how the car is to be sourced it will give the customer precise delivery data. All of the elements of that system are available to most car manufacturers, for instance most manufacturers would have an assembly line scheduling system, but the difference with this manufacturer is that the systems are integrated!

Generally, organizations are beginning to realize that in some instances value is to be gained from integrating the information available to the business rather than fragmenting it into functional subsystems. Interestingly such systems can cause the business to change its form of organization: departments can amalgamate and responsibilities can be reallocated in line with information movement.

---

information systems for competitive advantage.

At the detailed level this could be achieved in a variety of ways and hence organizations tended to move directly from Stage 2 towards one or more of Stages 3, 4, 5, 6 or 7. The logical sequence of the move from Stage 1 to Stage 2 did not continue forward towards Stage 3. In fact some organizations tried to move towards Stages 3, 4, 5, 6 and 7 all at the same time - not necessarily a good idea.

Stage 4: External efficiency

Turning to Stage 4, the boundaries of the business are widening. Organizations have realized that it is slow and inefficient to print out an order on paper and to post it to the supplier, just so that they can rekey it into their computer. Computers owned by different organizations are connecting to form networks which overcome these inefficiencies. Orders, invoices, product specifications and many other documents are being transferred electronically. This is very similar to Stage 1 because efficiency is the main benefit, but now it has an external and not internal focus. The term *electronic data interchange* is used to describe such systems.

Stage 5: External effectiveness

Just as Stage 2 involved using information collected in Stage 1, Stage 5, electronic information interchange, involves organizations in sharing information. For example, rather than two organizations carrying stock of a particular item it may be advantageous for the stock level of each party to be available to all interested parties. This is not just moving the electronic equivalent of paper between suppliers and customers, but the true sharing of information between different parties, to the mutual advantage of all.

Stage 6: External integration

Turning to Stage 6, sharing information can lead to a change in the form of who does what in an industry. Returning to Stage 5, the sharing of information on stock levels may lead to just one of the organizations keeping all the stock on behalf of all parties and having the information available to all. As in Stage 3, when it was said the internal form of the organization can be changed by information systems, so in Stage 6 the form of the industry can be altered. For example:

- customers can take on tasks traditionally undertaken by suppliers - such as raising the invoice on themselves; and

- suppliers can take on tasks traditionally carried out by their customers - such as raising purchase orders on behalf of the customer.

This is only possible if (in the first case) the customer has access to price information, and (in the second case) if the supplier has access to inventory information. Naturally, the parties concerned will have to negotiate the contractual arrangements whereby this can happen.

Summary

In most organizations today, Stages 1 and 2 best describe the way in which information systems are used, although the evolution of systems thinking is a continuous process and the edges may be blurred. Stages 3 to 7 are typically under development but are likely to be a relatively recent innovation.

The extent to which an organization has developed its thinking within this framework is a good indicator of its maturity. By understanding the application of information systems in this way it is possible to see the benefits that are being achieved, and the benefits that could be achieved in the next major phase of development.

Having considered various classifications of information systems and the way in which their application in business evolves, the next chapter examines the issues involved in their development and usage.

3

Issues in information systems

This chapter highlights and explores some of the issues involved in managing information systems. Rather than do this theoretically, it is done using an example that most of us can easily relate to.

Many people consider that success in the development of successful systems comes from technical excellence, because the constraints are seen as essentially technical. It is our view that while some of the problems are technical a substantial number are organizational and managerial; further, the proportion of managerial to technical problems is increasing and is likely to become dominant.

For many years the data processing department has been the scapegoat of organizational information problems. Sometimes the blame has been allocated correctly; however in some cases lack of direction from business management has caused problems to occur which manifest themselves in the data processing department. The identification of problems is vitally important to success. If the problems are of a technical nature then a better understanding of the technology is required. However if the problems are of a managerial nature, then the whole approach to resolving the problems will be substantially different.

This chapter first presents a situation, at length (see below). Then the issues revealed are analyzed from the viewpoints of the individuals involved. Finally, questions are posed which form a basis for the rest of the book.

John Long and Son is an organization involved in the design, production and marketing of some 2,000 different games to 20,000 retail outlets. The company employs approximately 5,000 people at two major sites in the United Kingdom. The company has been using computers for twenty-five years and has a substantial collection of applications in use. A central development and operation unit is located at one of the central sites which supplies service to the organization. This unit employs forty staff. Microcomputers have been in use for the last five years and approximately 150 are in use throughout the company.

The data processing department spends some 65 per cent of its development budget on maintenance, but on analysis only a small part of this cost is true maintenance. The majority is spent on small systems enhancement and one-off reports. In an attempt to deal with the issues of one-off reports a project code named 'Camel' was originated with the intention of downloading data from the central computer onto microcomputers for subsequent analysis. For this to succeed a number of the basic applications on the central computer require substantial modification. Potential users were invited to the launch of this project but it was poorly attended to the point of embarrassment. Those who did attend were disappointed to hear that the project would take thirty months to complete due to overstretched development resources and the substantial redevelopment required of basic systems. It was generally agreed, however, that such a facility was required and that the project should proceed.

Peter Walker, a bright regional sales manager with a master's degree in business administration (MBA), had long thought that if he could reanalyze the sales information, benefits might arise by linking together customers who traded under separate names yet were part of a large group. Such information was on the central computer, but not one of the sixty-eight sales reports available provided precisely the information required. He had heard on the grapevine that requests for new reports were being delayed substantially and sometimes such delays ran to twelve months! Peter had heard third hand that a new system due for delivery in three years had effectively stopped the development of new reports. However, business was a little quiet so Peter decided to try to develop this system himself. The first requirement was to obtain a microcomputer. This was not an easy task because all requisitions for such machines needed to be approved by the data processing department which always required detailed statements of requirements, costs, benefits and lots more information, most of which he did not have. Rather than tackle data processing, who no doubt would refuse his vague request, he consulted his brother, a civil servant who had an interest in computers. Taking the advice offered he went to the local computer store and purchased a laptop computer and a spreadsheet program. The official order specified a generalized piece of office equipment, but the computer store did not mind as long as they were paid! Peter put a great deal of effort into making the machine function but he put all this down to 'investment'. Slowly the analysis system came together, as a result of many hours of effort both at home and at work. However, Peter did not mind all this effort because he saw the task as a challenge. The rekeying of the sales data was tedious but for the moment he only did this for a very limited product range so that task was manageable. Some very interesting statistics were revealed by the analysis. His superior was impressed but was really only interested in the increased sales achieved, not in the system.

more ...

22

However, in the light of what they had learned it became obvious to both Peter and his manager that the system should be expanded to include all products and all customers. Peter knew his small computer was inadequate for such a task and so he interviewed three suppliers and chose a local branch of a national organization to supply a multi-user minicomputer with database software. It would have been very difficult to buy this machine, which was estimated to cost £25,000, without the agreement of data processing. He obtained the forms used when requiring a microcomputer and attempted to answer the questions, but even after his months of experimentation some were very difficult to answer. For instance, Peter was very unsure of the amount of management time that would be necessary to implement the system. However, he persevered even though this meant leaving many questions unanswered. In an attempt to involve the data processing department he requested assistance in completing the form, but the department was clearly offended that he had selected the hardware and software and was unhelpful. Two weeks after submitting the request a negative reply was received. Peter discussed this with his superior and it was resolved that Peter's superior would discuss the matter with the financial director, who was also responsible for the data processing department. The meeting was long and heated with the financial director asking for time for the new 'Camel' system to be completed. The sales department saw this as an unnecessary delay in receiving vital information. After much debate it was agreed that the sales department could proceed to implement the system as long as it did not affect any other system or other parts of the organization - an uneasy compromise!

Peter moved ahead very quickly purchasing the necessary equipment and software. The costs of the software escalated as the project progressed but this was seen as quite normal for an IT project because almost every other IT project the company had ever developed was delivered late and over the expected cost. However, within three months, the sales department had a six station multi-user database system operating, which was seen as a triumph having received little help from the data processing department. In fact Peter was planning other applications that could use the spare capacity on the sales department's machine and trained one of the office managers in the development of very simple enhancements and even small new systems. The data processing department allowed this office manager to work in the department for two weeks to become familiar with the procedures necessary to operate the computer.

Six months passed with no major problems occurring. At a routine meeting between the financial director and Peter's superior the new system came up again: it was agreed that part of an accounting system developed some years before by data processing could be discontinued because it was duplicated by the new system. This discussion lasted barely five minutes.

A further six months had elapsed when Peter received a call from this office manager informing him that a necessary backup of a file had not taken place and it was impossible to process the statistics without a major reprocessing of all the year's sales data. It was estimated this would take up to a month of continuous effort. This presented significant problems to the accountants because they were now users of the data, the duplication of which had been stopped six months previously. The data processing department could not recreate the old system because the necessary data were not available and hence the accountants had a significant problem.

more ...

When the matter was reported to the chief executive he professed ignorance of how computers work and claimed that nobody had even told him that the sales department had bought a computer. He was the chairman of the company's IT steering committee but had not attended any of its meetings for the past eighteen months. The reason he gave for this was that he did not understand the technical issues discussed at the meetings and hence considered his presence to be pointless.

The case study

The issues embodied in the case come out easily from an analysis of the different participants.

Chief executive

Data processing was not seen by him to be a major issue to the company and so he delegated the issue to the finance director whom he considered to be similarly uninformed. However, he knew the data processing manager was technically competent and paid him what he thought was a very large sum to look after such matters.

The chief executive felt he could not be a specialist in all matters, but objectively, he was in neglect of his duties. What evidence was there that many more opportunities were available within the company for the profitable application of information technology? Could it even be that the company's competitors were planning to use the technology to create advantage? Had the chief executive created an environment in which such ideas could surface and be tested? Had the chief executive used the IT committee to control the activities of the specialists and to be sure that the contribution to the company was consistent with company direction? Had the chief executive co-ordinated the activities of functional groups or had he allowed them to pursue functional goals? Had he even created a sensible organization structure - for instance, did it make sense for the data processing department to report to an uninformed finance director?

On all of these charges the chief executive was likely to be found guilty. You might think that no chief executive would ever control a company's IT activities in this way, but in the past such a separation of the IT activities from the business was not uncommon and the cynic would say that this attitude still prevails today.

Data processing

Turning to the data processing department, its staff may well see the problem beginning with users wanting to take over their role; for instance, they might ask why Peter could not wait for the 'Camel' system which was under development. They had created rules that attempted to restrict the use of technology to tasks that could repay the investment, yet these rules were broken with little consideration for the effect. Nobody seemed to support them, not even their ultimate superior the financial director. They were only consulted after all the relevant decisions had been made, even though they were supposed to be the specialists. They even tried to help by allowing an office manager to observe the running of their computer.

In summary, they may well hope that users have learned their lesson and will not attempt to do the jobs of others again. Such views could be expected in the circumstances, but what could the data processing staff be charged with? The rules of purchase appeared to be very restrictive - the prospective purchaser must know precisely what he or she wants and the exact benefits to be gained. It could be said that such rules would not encourage anything but the most straightforward of tasks which result only in labour savings. A second charge might be their unwillingness to be the minor element in a development team. Users 'doing it themselves' with just a little assistance from data processing staff is a growth area and quite a satisfactory method of development for some kinds of application. However, did the data processing department distinguish between application types? Nowhere was reference made to training being provided for users and it would be reasonable to expect this from a data processing department. Therefore, the data processing department was not blameless!

Peter Walker

Turning to Peter, he could argue that he nearly succeeded despite receiving little help from anyone. He developed and tested the prototype at great personal inconvenience. If he had followed the rules the innovation would never have got off the ground. Peter may consider that his only minor omission was not to train the operator who forgot to copy the lost data and even that was bad luck because the operator was a temporary employee standing in for the trained operator who was on maternity leave.

To be a little more objective, a number of his comments make a great deal of sense and he was an IT innovator in a non-innovative organization. However, he should have been willing to share his idea with the data processing department earlier and in more detail.

Peter's manager

Peter's manager would argue it was his job to provide facilities for his subordinates, and in this case it meant bullying the financial director into allowing Peter to continue to develop the idea. Therefore, in his own eyes he did a good job.

Objectively, he might reasonably be expected to understand something about sharing data between his own and other departments and to insist that Peter co-operate with others in producing the larger system. He did not do this because he was not interested in IT, but then he never had been and he had managed to progress quite satisfactorily to date - old habits take a lot of breaking!

Financial director

The financial director could be seen as the chief culprit. He was probably an accountant by profession and possibly quite a good financial director. In his own eyes the data processing department was 'allocated' to him.

He had allowed the development of the new system in an attempt to be flexible. If users want to be involved in systems development they must be allowed to do so - a comment he had no doubt heard at yet another 'hype' conference. He had stopped the production of the information in his own accounting department because it appeared inefficient to have two systems in operation producing similar data.

Objectively, he had allowed a basic company system to cease operation when he had little information on the robustness of its replacement. Flexibility is one thing, stupidity is another!

Issues to be managed

The John Long illustration outlines a situation in which every person involved appears to be trying to do their best but the outcome is catastrophic. What appears to be a technical matter, namely the failure to copy a file, is revealed upon examination to be more of a management problem. A number of questions have been posed which will be answered as the book progresses. These sorts of problems can sometimes be dealt with intuitively, but this is not the case for large or complex organizations.

A framework is needed within which these matters can be considered. Chapter 4 presents such a framework that will, if applied, ensure that the opportunities underpinning the business strategy are pursued - the chief executive of our fictitious company John Long should read at least this. Chapter 5 considers the tools which can be used to identify the opportunities available from IS - Peter, his manager and all the other managers within the organization would gain from also reading this chapter. Chapter 6 explains how each type of application can be best managed - the data processing staff, the chief executive and other senior managers would benefit from this chapter. Chapter 7 continues the theme of systems development and proposes a 'standard' process of development which can be tailored to suit individual needs. This would be of use to the data processing staff of our fictitious company, who appear to want to use the same development method irrespective of the type of application. Peter and similar managers directly involved with information systems projects would also benefit from this chapter. The following two chapters (Chapters 8 and 9) deal with some important background dealing with support and organization. All involved in management would benefit from these chapters.

Table 3.1   Summary of topics, issues and target audience

Chapter	Topic and issues	Appropriate to
Chapter 4	Strategy: how to underpin the business strategy with information systems	Chief executive and senior management
Chapter 5	Tools for strategic analysis: finding opportunities which will lead to advantage	All business management
Chapter 6	Framework for application management: how to approach the management of different kinds of application	All business management and data processing management
Chapter 7	A model for systems development: the process of developing and commissioning applications	Operational managers; IT management and staff
Chapter 8	Support: things that need to be managed well if applications are to succeed.	All management
Chapter 9	Organization for successful IS/IT.	All management

4

Integrating information systems and business strategy

Introduction

In the past the IS strategy of many organizations was essentially the summation of existing activities and plans, which themselves often derived from the bottom-up development of systems rather than a coherent business driven plan. This piecemeal approach to IS resulted in missed opportunities and an inefficient use of resources. Success or failure resulted from the organization's ability or inability to deploy technology in support of data processing or management information systems, without requiring any changes to the business or organization. However, this situation has now changed.

Today, the investments in systems and technology by outside parties - such as customers, suppliers and competitors - can require an organization to change its approach to managing IS/IT in order to avoid significant business risks and disadvantages. The lack of a coherent IS strategy can result in any number of the following problems:

1. Competitors, suppliers and customers may gain advantages over the organization.

2. Business goals will become unachievable due to systems limitations.

3. Systems are not integrated thus causing duplication of effort, inaccuracy, delays and poor management information.

4. Systems' implementations are late, over cost and fail to deliver expected benefits due to lack of clear focus on key business needs.

5. Priorities and plans are being changed continually producing conflict among users and IS staff, and poor productivity.

6. Technologies chosen do not integrate and even become a constraint to the business.

7. No means exist to establish appropriate IS/IT resource levels, to evaluate investments and to set Priorities consistently.

Therefore, in total greater expense than necessary is incurred to deliver less benefit than expected and IS/IT generates organizational conflict which wastes management time. These problems result in part from the inability of management to manage the demand for information or systems in accord with the business needs, and/or to manage the supply of systems and technology coherently, and/or to match the two successfully, as explained earlier in the book.

A strategy can be defined as '*an integrated set of actions aimed at increasing the long-term well being and strength of the enterprise*'. This chapter considers how the planning of IS/IT can become linked to the business planning process and hence driven by the management, in relation to the business environment and goals of the organization. Based on frameworks derived from general business strategy management, the ways of achieving the linkage are outlined. The need for effective organizational processes to establish the integration of IS and business strategies is also considered.

The context of IS/IT strategy

The business strategy of an organization is formulated by analyzing various external and internal inputs, by using a variety of techniques, to produce objectives, policies and action plans. Some of these processes will require the development or improvement of information systems. This statement of requirements (*what* needs to be done) must then be translated into technology-based solutions (*how* the needs could be satisfied). This basic linear relationship is shown in Figure 4.1, and is developed in Figure 4.2.

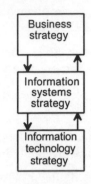

Figure 4.1 IS & IT strategy

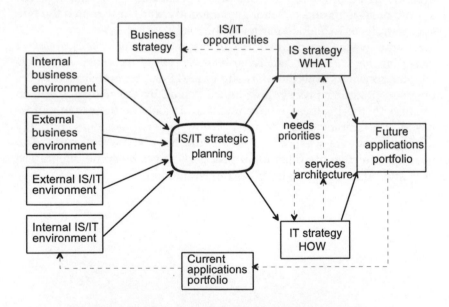

Figure 4.2 Inputs and outputs to IS/IT strategy

Even this simple logic is not always reflected in the reality of the IS/IT planning of many organizations - the process is often driven from the bottom up by technologists. However, as Figure 4.2 shows, IS/IT can and should be considered in the process of formulating strategy, in terms of what it can enable the business strategy to be. The potential impact of IS/IT on the enterprise in its business environment will depend not only on what it wishes to do, but also on what others are doing or are capable of doing. Integrating IS and business strategy must, therefore, include ways of assessing the potential impact which IS/IT can have on the organization and its business environment. This is just as important as considering other external environmental factors in formulating the business strategy. Techniques for carrying out such an assessment are considered in the next chapter.

Based on this IS/IT input and other considerations such as markets, services, products and resources, business strategic analysis should identify areas for potential IS investment. Whether or not they are achieved will depend on how well those business requirements are converted to actual information systems and how well they are delivered through the IT strategy. Clearly the whole process is a continuous one, like any aspect of business strategic management, requiring monitoring and updating as results are or are not achieved and as other business parameters change.

The two components of an IS/IT strategy are therefore the *information systems strategy* and the *information technology strategy*.

Information systems strategy

An information systems strategy defines the information and systems needs for the business and its component functions. If the organization consists of more than one business, then each business will define such a strategy and in addition there will be a strategy for satisfying corporate requirements.

The IS strategy should define what information systems the business needs for the foreseeable future, based on an analysis of the business, its environment and the general business strategy. The objective is to establish the demand for IS/IT applications, aligned closely to the business plans and issues. These needs will change over time and the demand must be updated continually, reviewed and prioritized based on business imperatives.

It may not be feasible to satisfy all these requirements, economically or technically, in the short term but over time more applications become feasible. The strategy must also define who, in organizational terms, is to be responsible for planning, delivery and implementation of the required information systems.

Information technology strategy

An information technology strategy defines how the needs will be met based on the priorities in the IS strategy and the information technology required to develop and operate existing and future applications. This involves determining how applications will be delivered and how technology and specialist resources will be acquired, used, controlled and managed in support of achieving the business needs. It will describe the activities which need to be performed and how they are to be organized, and it will thereby provide foundations for the definition and execution of projects which will ultimately achieve the supply.

Balancing demand and supply

A corporate or general management responsibility is to balance the demand and supply issues to ensure that the business plans are achievable. This will require continuing reconciliation based on business priorities and supply constraints. In order to do this the organization must establish a process which brings together business and IS/IT planning activity, and the products that they produce.

IS/IT strategic planning - a process framework

While the IS/IT strategic planning process is ongoing and iterative, during each stage of strategy development or re-evaluation it is important to have a consistent framework which is understood by everyone involved. The products of the process are IS strategies for the business which define its needs and priorities, and IT strategies for the data processing department which describe the requisite infrastructure and delivery services. The conjunction of these two products is a portfolio of future IS/IT applications which will satisfy the business requirements.

To achieve the required outputs the planning process must incorporate all the necessary inputs. The old computer adage 'garbage in, garbage out' (GIGO) applies to strategy development as much as to a single computer program. Comprehensive, reliable and relevant inputs - together with some innovative creative thinking - are required to identify the best courses of action.

The key inputs

The four relevant inputs have already been shown in the context of the overall process (see Figure 4.2 above). They are discussed in more detail below. This chapter also considers how the overall process of strategy planning should be managed to ensure its long-term effectiveness.

Some of the tools and techniques of IS strategic planning are then discussed in more detail in the next chapter.

The external business environment

This input is an assessment of the forces which are affecting the industry in which the business operates: the economics of the industry, its structure and competitive basis and within that the particular issues and pressures facing the business. This should normally be part of the strategic analysis of the business, rather than part of an IS/IT strategic planning process. Based on such an assessment, the role that IS/IT is playing or could play in changing any aspect of the industry can be examined. This then leads to the identification of potential opportunities or threats.

For example, the increasing power of retailers over manufacturing companies has been enhanced by retail point-of-sale systems and the information these provide for the retailer. Manufacturers need to consider how their IS/IT might be developed to either counter that pressure or perhaps better understand the potential of retail systems to gain some mutual benefit.

In the more general case, business environments are changing ever more rapidly, in some cases faster than the lead time for developing new systems. That speed of change needs to be reflected in reduced systems development lead times, which in turn will determine many aspects of the IT strategy - just as increasingly competitive environments impose constraints on product development lead times, and hence the methods of product design and manufacture.

The external IS/IT environment

An organization needs to understand two aspects of the external IS/IT environment: what new technologies are being developed, and how they are being used by others.

New technologies

The organization needs to appreciate and interpret the developments in information technology, and the trends in both the economics of its use and the practicalities of applying new technologies to its business needs. An understanding of the different sources of new technology and the available products will enable new application opportunities to be identified which may be appropriate to business needs.

Technology trends and developments need to be evaluated, both to select short-term options with a view to the long-term implications and also to plan when it looks most appropriate to intercept a new technology. When, for instance, would it be most appropriate to consider introducing electronic mail or image processing? No expressed need may exist but the cost of other forms of communication and document management must be compared over time with the ever improving economics of the new technologies.

All new technologies imply some risk and a learning curve for the business. Early understanding, interpretation and selective use of developing technologies may enable a future advantage to be identified and obtained. How many organizations did not consider the long-term implications of personal computers? The result of this misunderstanding has often been excessive direct expense plus enormous, often hidden, organizational costs. If the need for more rapid development of new systems is not identified in time, the learning curve for adopting new systems development tools may be too long to improve the business situation. Often, the short-term expediency to continue using known technologies and tools continually overrides the long-term need to migrate to more appropriate technologies.

Use of technology

More specifically, an organization needs to know how information technology is being employed by others within the industry, to what purpose and with what success. In fact, knowledge of the use of IS/IT in other industries can provide a source of good ideas which can be transplanted. It is important that an organization understands the business implications of what its competitors, customers and suppliers are doing with information technology.

Manufacturers of retail goods took a long time to appreciate the business implications of retailers' use of point-of-sales systems, bar coding and electronic data interchange. They have had to react quickly to pressures from their customers, often at great cost. A very successful flower auction suffered a short-term set-back when one of its competitors offered buyers the ability to buy flowers remotely through viewdata terminals. The competitor increased its potential market and in the short term attracted buyers away from the auction, until the auction responded with a similar system.

This illustrates not only the need to consider available technologies but also how they can be applied in an industry. In practice most companies which have gained strategic advantage from IS/IT have not used the 'latest' technology - it is too risky. They have innovated in a *business* sense, but used proven and well established, 'adequate' technology.

The internal business environment

This input consists of an analysis of information and systems needs based on what the business does, how it does it, and how it is organized and managed. Such an analysis must be related to the external business environment and, again, this should be done as part of the business strategic planning process. It will be concerned with the business mission, activities, capabilities and structure.

Mission and objectives of the business

The mission and objectives of the business must be expressed clearly, together with the strategies being pursued in order to achieve them. They will need to be interpreted accurately to define information and systems needs and also to set investment priorities.

Often, an organization's stated objectives and strategies are rather vaguely expressed and not well understood by all the management. Unless these are more clearly defined the resulting IS/IT strategy will be equally vaguely focused and become subject to 'flavour of the month' changes which will continually disrupt the planning and implementation of key systems.

Business activities

The business activities must be analyzed and the relationships and interdependencies understood. This analysis must be as independent as possible of the current organization structure.

It should describe the main processes of the business which enable it to provide customers with products and services, as well as what needs to be done to control and develop the business. This will lead to the definition of a business information architecture, which should be robust enough to accommodate any changes in how the business is conducted and organized.

The same analysis may well reveal weaknesses in the current organizational allocation of activities which either better systems can address or which cannot be addressed without organizational change.

Once this activity model is established it provides a basis for economic analysis, especially of the way in which business activity drives costs and generates added value. From this it is possible to identify areas of high potential benefit, by using new systems to reduce costs or increase value adding.

Strengths and weaknesses

The strengths and weaknesses of the business, and the reasons for these, need to be assessed and agreed. This process will include an analysis of the resources of the business - for example, financial, people, products, technology etc. - in order to identify where IS/IT can focus on exploiting the strengths and redressing weaknesses.

Structure and style

While the ideal information and systems model should be derived from a logical view of the business activities within the industry context, the eventual systems will have to be appropriate to the physical structure and style of the organization. Hence it is important to understand how the organization functions and how decisions are made in both the formal structure and the informal network of interpersonal relationships. This understanding will determine the type of information needed, who will need it and how it is presented and used.

Many management information systems fail to produce any benefits because they are too structured and fail to support informal decision making, which is based on interpersonal trust rather than the formal exchange of information. Equally, the rate of change of both organization structure and senior personnel will determine the type of system and information required. While no system will ever be flexible enough to cope with all the complexity and variety of organizational relationships, the structure, culture and style of the management will determine how information systems are structured and developed to support the management processes.

The internal IS/IT environment

An IS/IT strategy analysis needs to take account of existing systems and technology resources. Even information itself should be regarded as a resource with strategic significance.

Business systems and information resources

The business systems and information resources which are in place and currently being developed must be assessed according to their contribution to the business. These need to be analyzed in terms of how effective they will be in the future, not in terms of historical needs (Chapter 6 discusses in more detail how this assessment can be made by the business management.) The business strengths and weaknesses of existing systems (the 'current applications portfolio' in Figure 4.2) must be understood fully before further developments are undertaken, otherwise they may fail due to the inadequate foundations on which they may be built.

IS/IT assets and resources

The IS/IT assets and resources need to be catalogued and examined in order to determine whether the current capability and technology of the organization are adequate for future needs. This is not just an audit of current technology (hardware, software etc.) but also a review of the people, their skills, how they are managed and the methods used to develop and support the systems and underlying technologies.

One of the main reasons why IS/IT strategic planning studies often fail to deliver the changes required is that the organization is not capable of implementing the plans, due to lack of resources, skills or management process. One key aspect is understanding the culture and style of the IS/IT department and how it relates to the business culture. This reconciliation of the IS/IT approach and attitudes within the business environment is a critical aspect of IS/IT strategy development.

Summary of strategic inputs

In describing and analyzing each of these main inputs it is vital that agreement is reached among senior management so that everyone is working on the same basis. Equally, issues and problems that may arise should not be glossed over: they should be stated explicitly and become targets for resolution during the strategic planning process. If issues and problems are ignored at this stage they will re-emerge later and harm the implementation of the plans.

Processes for managing the strategy

Any strategic management process consists of three main stages and must incorporate two essentially different approaches. The three main stages are summarized in Figure 4.3.

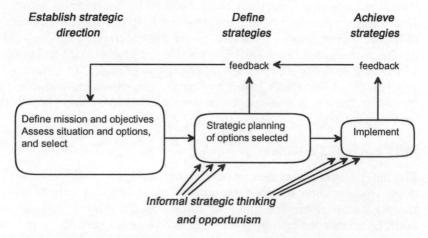

Figure 4.3　Strategic management processes

The approach may be formal or informal. The balance between the two enables creativity and ability lower down the organization to find the best way of achieving the objectives and strategic direction defined by the senior management. [2]

---

[2]　In Japanese industry in 1987, 2 million employees made 48 million suggestions which were implemented; this is many orders of magnitude higher than in British companies. Employee suggestions can improve what is done or how it is done within the strategic direction the management have set.　A suggestions scheme formalizes what would otherwise be an informal and haphazard process.

Strategic direction

The first stage of the process establishes the strategic direction. It defines objectives and selects the means by which that direction will be achieved.

For example, a major manufacturing company defined its strategy as doubling its sales and profits in five years by means of organic growth in the United Kingdom, acquisitive growth in Europe, producing high quality products and providing the best customer service levels within the industry.

This first stage needs to be understood and agreed formally at the highest levels within the company. It must also be endorsed by major stakeholders (in the example this was the parent holding company).

Strategy definition

The second stage is to define specific strategies for the main areas of the business (for example marketing, distribution, manufacturing and R&D) and turn these into viable plans by adding creative, informal thinking so as to identify the best way of achieving the strategy over time.

Obviously there must be feedback to ensure that over time the plans do take the company (and the functional units within it) in the required direction. While going through the strategy definition it will be helpful to understand how ideas and suggestions can be passed back to the direction-setting process.

Implementation

The third stage is to implement the plans in order to achieve the strategy. To some degree or another this involves everyone in the organization. The way the plans are to be implemented will be refined and improved by identifying new opportunities or better means of achievement, and we find that once again feedback is required. Control is also needed, for example to ensure that 'local' adaptation is still enhancing the overall strategy, not deflecting or undermining it. To succeed, all of the organization's energy must be focused in the desired direction. Without successful implementation strategic planning produces little benefit except perhaps the prevention of some wasted developmental effort.

The approach to strategic management

All that has been said above in general terms about devising and implementing business strategies applies equally to the IS/IT components of those strategies. This means that mechanisms must be in place to establish formally the required direction, plan the developments, resource requirements, and then implement the business systems and supporting technologies according to a plan.

The nature of the process

Too often in the past the strategy has been driven in reverse. For instance, IS and IT projects were defined, built up into a plan and presented to management for ratification as a 'strategy', but without reference to the business strategy. Relatively informal thinking has dominated due to a lack of direction and a lack of appropriate IS/IT strategic analysis tools.

However, the informal processes must not be stifled by a rigid planning process. Many of the most innovative uses of IS/IT which have resulted in competitive advantages originated as opportunistic ideas from quite low down the organization. The feedback loop must therefore also enable these ideas to reach the direction-setting process since they may result in advantage. The innate creativity in informal thinking can make a significant contribution to strategy.

The role of management

Senior management must initiate the process, set the direction and then demand feedback on progress. At the same time they must be receptive to new strategic opportunities, whatever means are adopted to actually devise and then manage the IS/IT strategy. They also have a responsibility to signal any change in direction at the earliest moment to avoid major projects proceeding apace when the business reasons for which they were required are no longer valid.

While senior management must initiate the process it is also critical that line management incorporate the IS/IT plans into their more detailed functional plans. The newer, strategic uses of IS/IT discussed in Chapter 2 (see Figure 2.4) require business managers not only to identify and evaluate, but also to manage new developments through to successful achievement of strategic benefits. This success will depend upon related business and organizational changes which must be planned and implemented carefully. This all demonstrates that line management and middle management must be involved actively and continuously in the planning and control of IS/IT implementation.

Establishing the IS/IT strategic planning process

IS/IT strategic planning must become a continuing process integrated with business planning, but two major problems remain for an organization wishing to achieve this long-term aim for the first time:

- *How to approach the development of the strategy and with what level of organizational grouping, in order to identify most precisely the business needs?*

  The business and IT people who will implement the strategy must own it and hence must be involved actively in its development and understand its implications.

- *How to carry out the process to develop the initial strategic plan?*

  The process must be manageable, both in terms of scope and duration, and it must deliver valuable results throughout the process, not just at the end. There must be clear checkpoints where agreement is reached, and management endorsement should be obtained before continuing more detailed analysis and formulation.

Both of these problems remind us that whatever approach is adopted all parties, including senior management, line management and IS/IT professionals, must be educated before the start as to:

- what is involved,
- how it is to be achieved, and
- what the expected products are to be.

A lack of mutual understanding and agreement on the objectives of the study at the start is a frequent cause of failure of such studies.

Business units

Addressing the first problem means that a coherent unit of the business has to be chosen for which an effective strategy can be developed. As with the development of business strategy, the appropriate level at which to develop a strategy is for a *business unit* (see Figure 4.4). A business unit can be defined as '*a component of the corporation that sells a distinct set of products or services, serves a specific set of customers and competes with a defined set of competitors*'. This may imply that organizational units need to be subdivided or even amalgamated in order to achieve a suitable strategic planning grouping, namely strategic business units. The starting point is taking an external view of what the organization does, not how it is structured to do it. This will enable the study to discover the particular business needs for information and systems within the business environment. Additional organizational needs can then be added to the basic requirements.

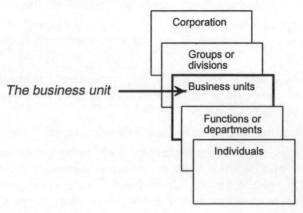

Figure 4.4   Appropriate level at which to develop IS strategies

Many companies are not organized into business units as described here. The component businesses may not be defined clearly within the organization structure due to historical or geographical reasons, or the use of the management talent available. It is important in the IS planning process to consider the logical strategic business units that the company comprises. Then the various techniques described later can be employed most beneficially.

For example, a large house builder had three divisions - Southern, Northern and Scotland - but in each division it built two main types of home, namely low cost starter homes in large numbers and executive homes on small select sites. The information systems needs for each of these two strategic business units were different because of the differences in design process, acquisition of sites, market place, cost structure and use of contractors and so on. In addition each divisional manager needed systems to manage the region's activities profitably.

Identifying and resolving conflicts

As has been said IS/IT strategy has traditionally been an amalgam of lower level functional, departmental or even individually determined plans for systems and technology driven mainly by internal, often localized, issues. Some organizations have attempted to develop corporate IS/IT strategies from the top down. However, the task is either too complex and hence takes too long, the business needs are too various or the environments are changing at different rates - all of which makes it difficult to develop a strategy that suits each component business unit.

Equally importantly, the business unit managers do not own an imposed strategy. Even at a group level, unless the business units comprising the group are almost identical, considerable compromises are needed to achieve any common strategies. The net result is usually that only the lowest common denominator of needs is met by the strategy. This tends to omit the key areas of the business and focus investments on accounting, personnel and other less critical business areas.

Consider the case where the same company has three different business units, dealing with:

- Unit A: Manufacturing for stock, in high volumes for many customers

- Unit B: Making to special customer orders, in low volumes for few customers

- Unit B: Supplying spare parts to all customers, and to others who bought original equipment from other sources.

Some key issues might be:

1. An invoicing system initially developed for Unit A (making for and selling from stock) has been adopted by Unit C who have added standard codes for the spare parts in the same way as product codes were already used by Unit A. No problems.

2. Unit B is told that they must also use the invoicing system but they can see no way to bill for variable design and engineering service costs, and they do not want any discount calculations which are built in for automatic calculation.

3. Unit C then decide that they wish to provide maintenance service as well as spares, and they find the same problem.

4. Unit A decide on an order processing system as a high priority, but they require pre-invoicing (before despatch) and this is not possible without major amendments to the system

An application which seems simple enough - invoicing - has become a problem for each of the three business units that wish to have it. Not only does a very complex situation threaten in terms of supporting the various versions of the invoicing system, but also each unit cannot achieve its ideal system without the agreement of the others. In the long term, therefore, the costs increase dramatically and benefits may be reduced. In effect, the strategy has been driven by IT supply issues (especially short-term economies) rather than IS demand side issues.

Within any large corporation different business units may well be adopting fundamentally different strategies which will require quite different emphases in the information and systems required. Michael Porter identifies two principal ways in which a business can achieve long-term success: 'low cost' and 'differentiation'.[3]

- In a unit striving for lowest cost in its industry sector, IS/IT will be targeted at cost reduction primarily through simplification and automation.

- For differentiation, while cost control is still important, IS/IT investment will focus on enhancing that differentiation through such things as speed and quality of service.

For instance, to achieve low cost a standardized order entry mechanism will minimize order handling costs. To achieve differentiation from competitors in the perception of the customer, it may be best to have a variety of ways of accepting orders, in ways which suit different types of customers. Equally, different policies for stock management will be required to carry out the different generic strategies.

All of this leads to the obvious conclusion that different IS/IT strategies will be required for businesses in different industry environments, pursuing different objectives by means of different business strategies. If two different business units are following different strategies - for example, one low cost, the other differentiation - then sharing systems would probably mean neither could pursue its strategy effectively.

The overall IS/IT strategy for the corporation will be the composite of the strategies of the units, plus the needs of the corporate and/or group business unit for information and systems. These will be based

---

[3] Porter, M.E., *'Competitive Advantage'*, Free Press, 1984.

on the means by which they develop, direct and control the total business. There may also be synergistic opportunities across the business units which can be identified from a higher level viewpoint, especially where the businesses are similar and/or trade with one another.

The IS strategy needs to be clearly focused on the particular, even unique, aspects of the business in its environment. When considering how the systems are to be supplied there may be further benefits in terms of economics and effectiveness of delivery by limiting the variety of IT strategies adopted, but this should involve the minimum number of business compromises from their ideal needs. Again if the strategy is predominantly driven by IT supply optimization issues, the business users will not own the strategy, nor will it meet their needs.

The first iteration

The means by which the first iteration of the IS/IT strategic planning process is carried out will undoubtedly influence the longer term strategic management approach - for better or worse. In the worst case a planning study can produce nothing of business value even after a considerable time and at great expense. The majority of strategic studies may not be that wasteful and ineffective, but many do not deliver much of real value and do not establish a viable mechanism for the future.

Some of the main reasons why such strategy studies fail are as follows:

1. Top management commitment to implementing the plan cannot be obtained.

2. The planning exercise takes too long for management to sustain interest - it is also very expensive and takes up too much of the management's time.

3. The process produces an overwhelming amount of detail which is difficult to interpret.

4. The resulting plan fails to spell out resourcing and financial implications.

There seem to be three main approaches adopted for strategic IS/IT planning studies, namely:

1. Set up a special IS/IT planning function to carry out the task. This is normally located within the IT department, which then owns the strategy!

2. Employ consultants to bring in techniques and skills to facilitate the process. This is obviously helpful, but in many cases the consultants take over and produce the strategy in the form of a large detailed report, and again ownership is lost.

3. Set up a task force or steering group to carry out the task, preferably led by an experienced and respected business manager. While being the most difficult approach to establish, it is by far the best, since not only does the strategy belong to the organization, but also it is more likely to be truly business driven, be carried out efficiently, and likely to be implementable.

The third of these approaches is the one most likely to overcome the main reasons why such strategy studies fail.

Following the first iteration, a longer-term approach needs to be established. Ideally IS strategic planning should become an integral part of the business planning process. The IT strategy should be an appropriate set of responses to those business IS strategies. In addition an ongoing management steering mechanism will probably be required to solicit feedback and to reconcile the demand and supply issues which will arise from time to time.

Summary

At the start of this chapter it was argued that unless an organization has a strategy for its information and systems which is driven by the business requirements, a number of problems will ensue. These could result in the business being seriously disadvantaged within its business environment, and/or spending significant sums on IS/IT investments, but achieving few business benefits. That strategy must prioritize demand according to business needs and then ensure that the supply of resources and technology is managed in the best way to satisfy the demand.

To achieve a coherent IS/IT strategy the organization needs to establish a business driven IS/IT planning mechanism. The timeframe of the resulting strategic plan should reflect the business planning horizon - this can be five years or more in a stable business, but may be only one to two years in a volatile one. In most businesses achieving a two to three year IS/IT strategic plan would be most appropriate. However, the planning mechanism must ensure that it is a rolling plan which is updated regularly (or even continuously) as achievements do (or do not) occur, as the business situation evolves, and as options change.

This chapter has described in general terms the context and concepts of IS/IT strategic management. The next chapter describes a number of the tools and techniques which can be used by senior, line and IS management, working together, to identify what information and systems the business needs to gain the greatest benefits and maximum leverage from the opportunities which IS/IT offers.

5

Identifying business advantages from information systems

Introduction

The previous chapter described the business strategic context within which information and the systems required can be identified and then managed successfully. No matter which process is chosen to establish the requirements some tools or techniques will be required to analyze the business, its environment, strategy and activities, and to select the areas where IS/IT offers benefits. However, the tools and techniques are only a means to an end, they are not a substitute for creativity and experience. Properly used they will encourage creativity and focus experience and intuition, leading to successful future actions.

The objective is to determine business applications of IS/IT which are relevant and which will improve business performance. This may involve improvements in the efficiency of operations, in the quality of the management processes and even in the way the business is conducted or organized. In some cases all three levels of improvement may be evident.

This chapter considers some high level techniques which can be used to identify the demands for IS, based on the current business imperatives and longer-term potential opportunities. It is not an exhaustive or exclusive set of ideas but a set of tools and techniques which can be used by management, users and IS specialists together to achieve an agreed view. No strict methodology for using the techniques can be defined which suits every set of business circumstances, but a planning framework will be described within which the ideas can be applied when the principles underlying them can be understood.

The framework brings together three aspects of demand planning which need to be considered simultaneously. It thereby enables the resulting requirements to be reconciled and the most valuable selected for action. The three aspects of the approach are as follows:

- current situation appraisal to decide 'where we are now' in terms of the business, the information systems currently in place and their relevance in the future;

- creative future opportunity 'spotting' to identify what the business could do with IS/IT - i.e. 'where we could be';

- analytical assessment of what the business needs to do more immediately with IS/IT if it is to achieve its current business plans and objectives - i.e. 'where we want to be'.

The result is a portfolio of information systems requirements which comprises:

- a business-based review of the value of existing or past IS/IT investments,

- a set of known requirements to be satisfied in the near future, and

- a set of potential longer-term IS/IT opportunities.

The next chapter (Chapter 6) then considers how supply side strategies can be established to satisfy the variety of demands.

A planning framework for determining the requirements

The framework shown in Figure 5.1 describes the key steps involved in defining comprehensively the IS requirements for a business - i.e. the applications portfolio to be managed now and in the future. The process is not as complex as it might first appear, but before considering the use of the various tools and techniques within it the rationale for the framework structure needs to be explained. It illustrates and details the three aspects of the approach mentioned earlier: situation appraisal, analytical opportunity analysis and creative opportunity analysis. The framework is intended to be used to determine the requirements for a business unit as described in the

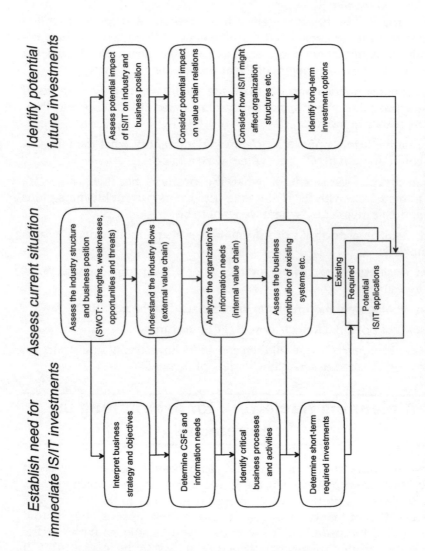

Figure 5.1 An approach to identifying information systems opportunities

previous chapter. By using the same framework for all units in a corporation, however, additional opportunities can be identified, as will be shown here.

Situation appraisal

The first stage in the process is essentially an extension of the situation appraisal required for developing a business strategy or plan. It poses questions as to whether improved information or systems could be used to affect directly the environment within which the business is operating and specifically the various competitive forces acting upon the business. This implies considering options available to the business and also to its competitors, customers and suppliers, and how those options might gain a relative advantage for any or all of the participants.

It is essential to consider the strengths and weaknesses of the various parties in the industry in terms of their ability to take advantage of IS/IT. This leads to identifying potential opportunities and threats based on the potential impact which IS/IT could have on the industry and the balance of competitive forces. The situation can then be assessed in more detail using *value chain analysis* to identify the key information flows in the industry and how the balance of influence could be changed along the supplier-buyer links in the chain to gain an advantage:

- the *external value chain* understanding can lead to opportunities to link the business more effectively with the outside world by means of its information systems, the benefits of doing so and the consequences of not doing it.

- the *internal value chain* is a way of identifying the main information needs and flows associated with what the business does, rather than how it is organized to do it.

Hence an ideal information and process model can be established as a basis for achieving the appropriate information and systems integration. This may lead to changed organizational relationships in order to exploit the new ways in which IS/IT can enable the business to operate or be managed. It is against this future model of the business requirements that the existing systems should be appraised, in terms of their functionality and how well they link the key related activities. What do the systems enable the business to do and what do they inhibit it from doing?

The product of this decomposition of the business relationships, activities and information-based processes will be a number of potential IS options for investment. However, this is not the whole picture, merely what could be done given enough time. What should be done in the next year or two depends on what the business wants to achieve in that period, and how it intends to achieve it. To do this the objectives and strategy of the business need to be interpreted to define short-term needs and select the priority areas from the ideas generated, namely those which could yield the earliest significant benefits.

Future needs and opportunities

This process is more analytical - a systematic review of the objectives to identify what is critical to achieving them and consequent information and systems dependencies. These critical success factors will lead to specific information needs and also identify the critical areas of business activity where improved systems will have the most benefit. Again it will expose weaknesses in the current information and systems which need to be overcome, if disadvantage is to be avoided. These will provide the criteria for selecting the key areas for immediate investment - i.e. the required plan of development, enhancement or correction. Other potential application ideas should not be rejected - some may well be worth further evaluation, even prototyping, and others may not be feasible in the short term but should be put 'on the back burner' for review in time or if certain business and technology factors change.

Each of the techniques is described in more detail below. This brief overview of the framework is intended to show how the techniques can be brought together to establish an overall picture of the IS options actually or potentially available to the business and their likely contribution. The framework enables a management assessment from a number of important aspects, as follows:

1. It enables the existing IS/IT applications to be valued in a future rather than historical context.

2. The affects of IS/IT on the industry can be considered before making internally based decisions.

3. Creative ideas for the use of IS/IT can be evaluated against an information-based model of the business in order to decide on their relevance and importance.

4. It ensures that the IS/IT investment plan is driven by the business objectives and not local priorities or purely IT considerations.

5. When external or internal factors change it will enable reassessment of any business or IS/IT aspect of the requirements.

Above all it is a business driven framework in which decisions about IS requirements can be arrived at and agreed by the business management. Its purpose is to establish a demand driven, opportunity seeking approach to the planning and control of IS/IT separately from considerations of supply. It is always important to decide what you want to do before deciding how to do it, although this has not always been the case in IS/IT planning.

Assessing the business position within the industry in terms of IS opportunities and threats

In developing a business strategy the various products and services of the business are normally assessed in terms of their particular market situations and their strengths and weaknesses compared with those of competitors.

The Boston box

Various techniques exist to make such an assessment. The simplest and most popular is the product portfolio matrix commonly known as the 'Boston box', whereby products are considered in terms of their relative market share and the growth potential of the market (see Figure 5.2). This is based on the concept of a product life cycle of four stages - emergence, growth, maturity and decline - during which the relationship of demand to supply in the industry changes. The types of information and systems required will change during this life cycle and hence it is important to support each stage differently.

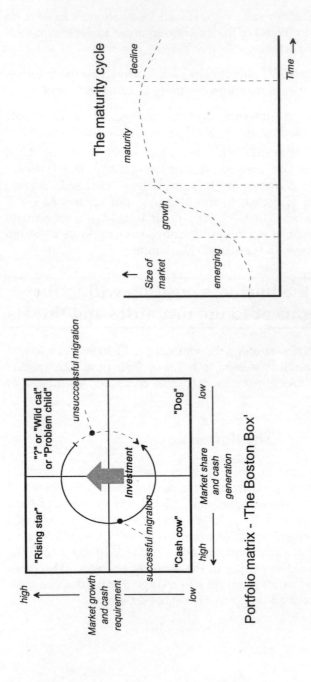

Figure 5.2   Business/product portfolio matrix

Emergence

With new or emerging products demand is very uncertain and the market is ill defined. Customer requirements need to be identified and matched with the product attributes and new channels of distribution may have to be developed. The information focus will be on market research and product development.

Decline

At the other extreme, in a declining market supply will be greater than demand, the market and competition will be well understood and the objective normally will be to be very cost effective in serving the broad market (or to be selective and serve profitable niches). The information required will be very detailed in terms of demand forecasts, profitability of customers and products, and all aspects of direct and indirect costs will need to be controlled very carefully, not only to maintain profitability but also to release resources to invest elsewhere in the business. The types of system at the two extremes of the life cycle are quite different.

Growth

In growing markets information needs will change gradually as demand ceases to exceed supply and competitive pressures increase. In the Boston box, successful products in growth markets are termed 'stars' and in mature markets they are called 'cash cows'.

Star products need major investment to meet the growth in demand, for instance in marketing capability, production capacity, new distribution channels and in revised supplier relationships. Equally there must be an investment in new or enhanced information systems to help meet the required growth, especially systems to identify and forecast demand and convert this into supply and resource requirements. Knowledge of costs and contribution to profit, changing customer preferences, service expectations and competitor activity will become important as the market begins to mature.

At this stage the market will become more competitive but initially the ability to satisfy a major share of demand is more critical than beating specific competitors. Systems must be able to support growth and must not inhibit the ability to satisfy demand. Good systems can also create barriers to entry by tying in customers and suppliers, and by making successful entry to the market dependent on the availability of these systems. The investment involved may be prohibitive.

Maturity

In mature markets, competitive rivalry will be intense and supply will gradually exceed demand. The primary objective is to retain market share and 'milk' the cash cow: the profits can be reinvested in new areas of product or market development.

This implies a more defensive investment strategy and IS can support this by enabling more accurate market segmentation, increasing productivity and optimizing working capital requirements (such as inventories) to match anticipated demand. Important considerations are:

- being more efficient and effective in using resources;
- better management of supply and distribution channels;
- building up customer switching costs; and
- an understanding of specific competitors' products, performance, strengths and weaknesses.

Pricing policies will become more aggressive and critical and these need to be based on good market and cost information. In general, much more detailed control and planning is required. In many companies, while the business issues resulting from the product and industry life cycles are well understood, the means to translate them into appropriate, sustainable, information systems is less well appreciated. Many companies try to force-fit existing systems to the high growth areas but they do not work well, because they were designed for mature products. Force-fitting systems from another part of the business at a different stage of development - or in a different market, or a different competitive situation, or even pursuing an inherently different strategy - reduces effectiveness and is all too common.

For example, a leading door manufacturer in the United Kingdom made two different types of doors:

1. Standard doors of some 200 designs sold through a catalogue to house builders and through builders' merchants. The door manufacturer had a high market share and produced several million doors per year. This could be defined as a cash cow in a low growth mature market. The competitors were well known.

2. Speciality doors such as safety, security and fire doors, and high quality or odd sized or shaped doors. These were made to specification in small batches but were very profitable and had a

reasonable market share. The competition was much more diverse and included imports from Holland and Germany. The customers were also more dispersed and each purchased far smaller quantities, but the market was growing quickly. These doors were the 'star' products.

The information systems had been developed to meet the needs of the volume business and were very effective in supporting a low cost strategy and the required automation, namely optimizing production, stock holding and delivery patterns. However, the systems did not really support the growing speciality door business where the objective was to differentiate the products on quality and service and hence justify a premium price. They had not been designed to support such a product range or customer base, but they were being used, ineffectively, to manage that part of the business. Consequently the available profit margins were not being achieved and customer orders were being lost. A more appropriate set of systems for this different and high growth area was needed.

In IS terms, the above door manufacturer needs to be considered as two strategic business units with different business strategies and requiring different information systems. From an IS perspective greater advantage can be achieved by considering the different business units and their specific needs individually; this would not always be the case from other perspectives, such as human resource management or financial management.

Porter's five forces

A further useful tool in such an analysis is provided by Michael Porter's approach to the appraisal of competitive forces in an industry to help define an appropriate overall business strategy. Figure 5.3 shows the key forces determining how an industry develops and which need to be assessed and interpreted if a business is to succeed in-the long term. Added to the basic diagram are some questions indicating how IS/IT might be used to assist in dealing with the various forces and to gain maximum advantage. The main objective is to ensure that IS investments are focused on aspects of the business which affect the competitive position directly. The first stage is to determine which of the forces pose a major threat to the future success of the business and in what way.

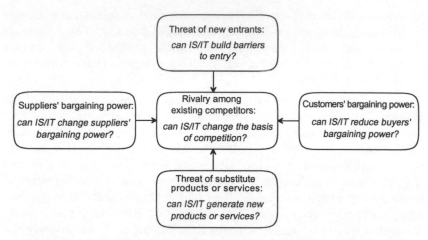

Figure 5.3   Analysis of competitive forces in an industry (after Porter)

Obviously IS investments are only one of many ways of dealing with the issues that arise. Having ranked the various forces in terms of intensity of impact and immediacy of threat, the most critical should then be considered in terms of how IS (perhaps in conjunction with other developments) could be used to gain advantage or avoid disadvantage. This requires that the organization also understands what competitors, customers and suppliers are doing or plan to do with IS/IT and what the effects might be.

Often the action required will involve a relationship between two or more of the forces. For instance, establishing barriers to entry might involve increasing customer loyalty, increasing their switching costs and/or tying in suppliers more closely or reducing their bargaining power and hence making entry more difficult. The relationship between suppliers, the business and the customers will then be considered in more detail in the value chain analysis, details of which follow later in this chapter.

Threat of new entrants

New entrants threaten that additional capacity will be introduced to the industry, the basis of competition may change and in the short term, at least, prices will be reduced. This can be counteracted in a number of ways by IS investments:

- Better control of distribution and supply channels to limit access.

- Segmenting the market to match the products of the business more accurately and providing a more complex target for the new entrants.

- Exploiting existing economies of scale more effectively to reduce costs in anticipation of a price war.

- Increasing the rate of new product innovation and development and/or differentiating existing products on quality or service.

In all these areas information systems can help by providing better information, greater efficiency and an ability to react faster, for example by the use of computer-aided design (CAD) in product design. The cost of the investment in systems will increase the entry threshold, as has happened over the last ten years in grocery retailing, travel and financial services.

Threat of substitute products or services

The substitute may be a direct replacement (such as air for sea travel), or an indirect replacement in terms of customer preference (such as a holiday for a new hi-fi). In either case the threat of substitution will take the market into decline and produce more intense price competition, especially where fixed costs are high. Again information systems can be used in a number of ways to counteract the threat including the following:

- Redefining market segments and products to match changing preferences and retain profitable areas.

- Improving the rate of product innovation to recapture preferences.

- Enhancing the products with new services to increase their perceived value.

- Improving the price/performance of the existing product by cost reduction.

- Identifying other new customer needs that can be satisfied, i.e. exploiting the existing customer base to develop new products.

Of course it would always be better to stay one step ahead by using the information available to identify changes in customer needs, to be proactive in developing new products or services, and to increase the breadth and depth of the product portfolio.

Rivalry among existing competitors

Where rivalry among existing competitors is intense, generally in mature and declining markets, the effects are likely to be fierce price competition, increasing buyer power, more rapid product enhancement, and distribution and customer service levels becoming critical. These produce an obvious conflict in terms of cutting costs and increasing service levels. Without effective information systems costs can easily increase in such circumstances and service levels can decline - the wrong product available at the wrong place and at the wrong price. Whatever IS is used for in this case, it must be deployed in support of the chosen business strategy - low cost, differentiation or niche marketing - in order to enhance that strategy effectively. For example:

- Identifying how IS can be used to reduce real costs across the board, in relation to competitors, in all activities and relationships in the business.

- Identifying how IS can enhance the type of differentiation sought, whether that be image, product quality, services provided - as perceived by the customer and end consumer.

Getting close to the end consumer as well as the immediate buyer is important in order to understand their requirements and increase their loyalty and/or fear of buying less good products elsewhere.

Many retailers in highly competitive markets, such as clothing and DIY, have realized that product range, quality and convenience no longer provide sufficient differentiation to induce customer loyalty. Hence they have added further services to induce the customer to stay with them. Some of these, such as discount cards and personal financial services are wholly dependent on the availability of information systems and information about the customers (e.g. where they live, who they are, what they buy and when).

Bargaining power of buyers and suppliers

IS can be used to improve the balance of power with buyers and suppliers. Ways to achieve this will be considered in more depth in the next section, but first it is worth summarizing the business effects when the power of each is high.

- When a *supplier* is in a strong position due to its size or the scarcity of what it provides, it can obviously increase prices, reduce the quality of what is supplied and make it less readily available, causing at best uncertainty and at worst an inability to satisfy customers profitably. 'For the want of a nail . . the war was lost', as the story goes.

- Equally when *buyer* power is high, due to size, lack of differentiation in products available, or over-supply, then prices will be forced down at the same time as a higher quality of product and service is being demanded by the customers and from the competing suppliers.

One approach is to make it easier for the buyer - by reducing the cost of buying rather than the price of the product - thereby generating mutual benefit. Value chain analysis is used to explore these ideas more thoroughly, and is described below.

The main purpose in this stage of the analysis is to focus attention on the business, in terms of its product portfolio and in relation to key external forces, and to identify the different ways in which IS could affect the relationships and competitiveness, not only of the firm but also others within the industry. This generates ideas and identifies whether current investments are supporting or undermining the chance of business success.

Value chain analysis

Value chain analysis is one of a number of techniques which enable management to analyze the role information plays in the industry, in the relationships between organizations and in the business itself. This can show the organization what information it needs to obtain, where that might come from and also how intra- or inter-organizational systems might improve its competitive position. Value chain analysis helps define business strategies in terms how the organization adds value and how it incurs cost. It helps to establish the position relative to customers, suppliers and competitors and how that position can be enhanced and sustained within the industry structure.

For every industry there is a value chain which shows how the end product (or service) is developed from raw inputs. The chain is a series of stages, each of which adds value and incurs cost. It is also a set of relationships between those organizations involved, each of which consumes resources of various types to produce value; this value is only realized when the evolving product or service is acquired by the organization at the next stage in the chain. The difference between realized values and actual costs is the margin of profit.

In every case a matching of supply and demand must occur at the various stages of the chain in order to provide the required product or service at an appropriate cost. Within any industry there is a finite demand in terms of how much of the product is required and how much will be paid for it, and also at any time there is a finite supply of materials and resources to produce the product or service. Organizations compete not only with companies doing much the same thing but also with others along the chain for a share of the revenue and overall profit available within the industry. That overall profit can be increased if demand and supply can be matched more accurately throughout the chain. Any business which operates at some distance from the eventual demand and also from the supply of key resources has to deal with considerable uncertainties and will find it difficult to optimize its performance. If, relative to its competitors, it can capture better key supply and demand information, it can optimize its performance relative to the competitors' uncertainties.

In non-profit making organizations or public bodies the income may not be generated by the services provided. Income is probably indirect, through donations or taxation. However, there is still a value chain and the organization's costs must be contained within the funds available. It may not compete for customers but it does compete for available resources.

This industry-level view of information highlights the key flows of information which the business needs to intercept and influence. This provides a basis from which its internal information and systems needs can be assessed and defined in more detail. Many industry value chains are very complex and involve manufacturers, distributors, service providers, sources of skilled staff and capital as well as raw materials, equipment and buildings etc. It is not necessary that a detailed model of all elements is produced, but the key dependencies and associated information which might affect the success or failure of the business within the industry structure should be the focus of attention.

The external value chain

Figure 5.4 depicts a simplified value chain for a manufacturing industry, and it illustrates issues which will be of concern to many organizations, whether in manufacturing or some other industry.

There is a continuous exchange of information going on throughout any industry chain but a single business is only a part of the whole and therefore has only a limited view. A large corporation may own businesses in more than one part of the chain - clearly such an organization has major opportunities to gain advantages over more focused rivals, by sharing information or by developing effective inter-company trading systems. However, in large corporations which are managed on profit centre lines, the links between divisions within a single firm are often considered to be external and this makes it harder to implement integrated systems. In other cases unitary companies work strenuously to develop close partnerships with their partners because they know that there are significant mutual advantages to be gained by firms linking their information and systems throughout the chain, irrespective of ownership.

Potential benefits

A number of long-term benefits arise as follows:

1. Given that at any time the industry can generate a certain amount of net profit, that profit is shared among the various organizations in the chain.

2. If, in the version of the chain which includes 'our business' the overall net profit can be increased, we can take an increased share of that profit and hence outperform our direct competitors.

3. Where demand and supply can be matched more accurately inter-organizational systems have a special contribution to make.

4. To do this normally requires the co-operation of suppliers or customers to provide that information and hence they would expect some benefit in return; it might also involve transportation service providers and banks where they are substantially involved.

5. If the benefit generated is shared with key customers and/or suppliers, then everyone can become more profitable provided they are an integral part of 'our' more efficient or effective version of the industry. For such systems investments to succeed, the benefits need to be shared in order to gain long term from buy-in to the system.

6. Because rival firms are competing for the same resources, suppliers and customers their position will be weaker. Suppliers will prefer to sell to 'our' business because they are more profitable when they do. Hence prices to competitors will increase and service levels

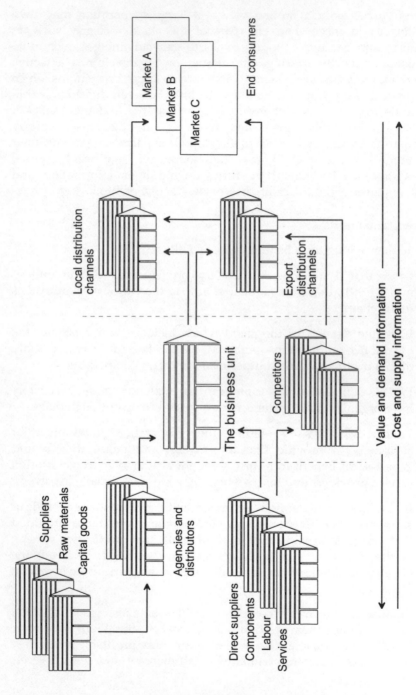

Figure 5.4   The external value chain

will reduce as their attention is diverted to achieve the new level of profit available by trading with us. Equally, customers will prefer to buy from us because of the lower overall cost of purchasing and will begin to demand lower priced products and better service from our competitors.

In the best case the net result is that our competitors face increased costs, poorer supply-side service levels, lower sales revenue at the same time that their customers demand higher service levels, leading to a long-term, sustainable advantage for our business. Of course, this sounds easier to achieve than it actually is and in most cases only part of the advantage may be realizable with only some suppliers and some customers.

Gaining the benefits

In order to understand how information systems can produce such mutual benefits consider any one interface between two organizations in the chain. The basic relationship is that of buyer and seller: placing orders, taking delivery, checking and eventually paying for the items. This involves considerable administrative cost and processing of data by both parties.

- These costs can be reduced by doing things only once, perhaps by using direct electronic data interchange (EDI) between each partner's computer systems. This can help by eliminating clerical effort, delay and potential inaccuracy.

- No doubt both parties hold stocks of the same items in order to satisfy demand or in case of supply problems. That duplication of cost can be eliminated by each giving the other access to stocks and by jointly planning requirements ahead of orders. This could even result in direct links between production and distribution scheduling systems to optimize resource use between the two organizations.

- Shared quality control systems can be introduced to avoid duplicate or inconsistent checking which would result in unnecessary cost and waste.

- New product designs can be developed in parallel using shared CAD systems to speed up the engineering processes.

- Payment systems can be optimized to ensure both parties avoid the need for expensive short-term finance.

In this way significant costs can be taken out of the interface and each partner is able to perform more effectively. The benefits are, in effect, mutual in the most literal sense of the word.

Examples

There are examples of all of these ideas, sometimes as a result of active co-operation but sometimes because a more powerful partner simply wanted it to happen.

DIY retailers have moved on from basic EDI transaction exchange to joint stock planning and optimized delivery logistics. Suppliers who cannot or will not co-operate have to find other outlets for their products.

A major oil company operates a joint stock management system with its main steel supplier at its North Sea depots. The stock belongs to the steel supplier but is used as and when required by the oil company and paid for as used - forecasts of demand enable the steel company to maintain appropriate stock levels at the depots.

Many retailers who have installed point-of-sale (POS) systems can exert leverage back through the chain by the knowledge of exactly what is bought and when, enabling them to hold the ideal range and quantities, and demand just-in-time (JIT) replenishment by suppliers. For further advantage, however, retailers need to know what is *not* bought and *why not*: for instance, because of lack of availability or too high a price. Identifying this further element of 'unfulfilled demand' or 'lost sales' is more difficult, but it is a help to both the retailer and the suppliers if it is identified and shared. The main danger is that when the co-operation is one sided and the benefits are all taken by the retailer, the supplier cannot survive. In the long term, however, reducing the number of potential suppliers will simply change the balance of power once more.

The situation is not always best resolved in such a direct systems relationship. A kitchen manufacturer built excellent internal systems which enabled it to outperform its rivals in terms of speed and accuracy of delivery to consumers' orders. The consumer dealt with a retail outlet which ordered the kitchen from a distributor, which in turn bought from the manufacturer. Initially the advantages did not materialize - the distributor was more interested in selling the stock held than encouraging the retailer to sell the products it could most easily order and hence held less stock of. Only when the retailer could share in the benefits of placing orders direct to the factory did sales increase. The distributor became merely that - someone who was paid to move the finished goods to the retailer or customer for fitting.

A timber importer identified a key factor which affected timber prices outside his immediate industry sector. The number of housing starts in the United States (mainly timber framed houses) determined how much Canadian timber was bought in the United States and hence in a three to six month timeframe how much timber would be available for export to Europe. A model was built which monitored the number of housing starts in the United States and could forecast likely timber prices several months ahead, giving the buyers a distinct advantage when negotiating with other sources.

As a final example, a lighting company provides lighting specialists with a computer system to help design lighting systems in new buildings. The designers do not buy the lighting systems but influence the contractors, who buy from wholesalers, who in turn buy from the manufacturer. By providing the computer system the manufacturer can ensure that its latest products are favoured by the designers who can easily convert the design into a specification and components list for the contractor. In turn the contractor can most easily satisfy the contract by buying the components from one wholesaler whom the manufacturer ensures holds stocks of the latest products in appropriate configurations to meet the designs.

Electronic data interchange as an enabler

This brief overview of external value chain analysis from an information perspective is intended to show how by examination of key flows of information in the industry, opportunities for advantage can be identified. As EDI becomes more easily and more extensively available it offers major advantages to those who can understand the changes in business relationships that it can bring about. Its use implies co-operation with others in the industry if the benefits are to be obtained - even co-operation with competitors in the development of standards.

Equally importantly, before considering the information and systems required within the organization, the detail of the external data exchanged with trading partners must be examined and agreed, so as to ensure the maximum level of integration with internal systems.

The internal value chain

The internal value chain shows how the various activities and functions in a business unit contribute to the customer's requirements, and how costs are incurred in so doing. Understanding what is done, how it is done and how business activities are related leads to a better understanding of information and systems needs and opportunities. The value chain helps to get beyond the detail of current arrangements in order to see the bigger picture in relation to the whole business and the way that customers see it. The original value chain model was based primarily on manufacturing business, but its structure can be applied to most other types of business. The model identifies two different types of business activity - primary and support - and provides a framework for organizing the detail within them.

Primary activities

Primary activities fulfil the value adding role of a business unit, as seen in its industrial context by its suppliers and customers. These primary activities must each be optimized individually and the whole linked together if the best overall performance is to be achieved.

The generic groupings of these activities can be considered in a sequence from supply side to customer side:

1. **Inbound logistics**: obtaining, receiving, storing and provisioning key inputs and resources required by the central operations of the business. This can include recruiting staff, buying materials and services, and dealing with subcontractors.

2. **Operations**: transforming inputs of all types into the products or services to meet customer requirements. This involves bringing together the requisite materials, resources and assets to produce the right quantity and quality of products or services - for instance in a university, delivering the courses in the prospectus and examining the students.

3. **Outbound logistics**: distributing the products or services to the place of sale, or to customers directly, using channels of distribution by which the customer can obtain the product or service and pay for it.

4. **Sales and marketing**: making customers and consumers aware of the product or service and how they can obtain it; promoting the

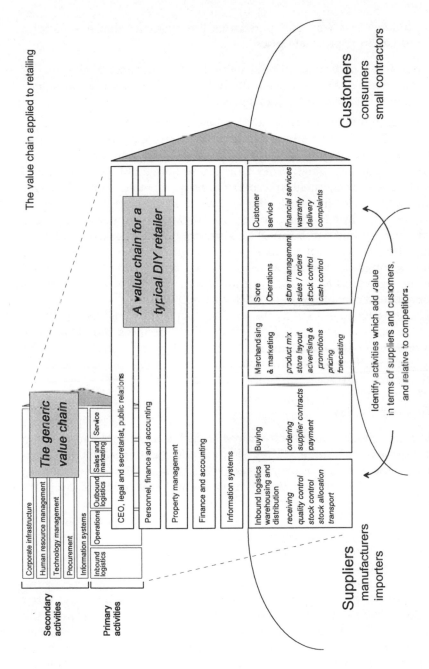

Figure 5.5 The value chain applied to retailing

products in a way that persuades the customer that it satisfies a need at an appropriate price.

5. **Services**: adding additional value for the customer at the time of sale or afterwards, for example by means of financial services, user training and warranty claims processing .

A value chain for a typical DIY retailing organization is shown in Figure 5.5. This shows how the generic groups can be re-interpreted and re-defined to provide a specific model of a non-manufacturing business. The groupings differ from those above but the rationale of the structure is consistent in terms of the supplier-to-customer linkage.

In other service industries the key value adding operations may be less obvious. In a building society for instance customer savings and mortgage lending can be seen as different businesses which relate to each other in terms of the use of the available funds. On the other hand, savings can be seen as inbound logistics (getting the money in) and mortgages as outbound (putting the money to work) while funds management constitutes the central core activity.

Deciding whether to view the primary parts of a business separately or together can be assisted by value chain analysis but it will not 'automatically' produce a decision. The value chain is just a vehicle for exploring options and understanding consequences: it helps to shape a discussion rather than prescribe a solution.

Support activities

Support activities are those required to facilitate, control and develop the business over time. They do not add value directly but only through the enabling of primary activities. Examples are: accounting, personnel, information systems, research and development, property management and legal services.

In a multi-business unit organization some of these support activities may be common, the degree of sharing depending on similarities between the units and the economies or other benefits gained.

In many ways a business does not always have much choice over what its primary activities are, since they are heavily influenced by the nature of the products, customers and suppliers in its industry. What *is* critical is how well it carries out each activity and how it links the activities together, so as to maximize the margin between value added and costs incurred. Information intensive activities such as forecasting, capacity planning, scheduling, pricing and costing must be linked throughout the chain if each stage in the internal value is to make the best contribution to the overall result.

However, a business does have control over how it carries out its support activities. They can be shared centralized services used by all business units or delegated activities within each of the units. It is a matter of choice, bearing in mind the need for managerial consistency across the units and the particular business situation and unique aspects of each unit. Either way, the support activities have two main contributions to make:

1. To enable the primary activities to be carried out at optimum performance levels, for example by providing required services or by the development of new products, technologies or resources to meet current and future business needs.

2. To enable the business to be controlled and developed successfully over time, principally through support for the management and through improved methods of planning and control.

Support activities that are not well managed themselves can actually disrupt the smooth running of the business by spreading their tentacles of control throughout the primary activities - consider the 'sales prevention system' often referred to by marketing people, or just 'the system' which is so often seen as a barrier to business rather than a support.

Use of the internal value chain

It is important to understand the cost drivers in a business and why and how they are managed. The value chain model offers a useful way of identifying these drivers and allocating all the real costs in order to identify where savings can be made, and where performance needs to be improved. Continuing investment in one area (for example manufacturing productivity) is pointless unless other areas are improved (such as sales forecasting and inventory management). All costs derive from activity of some kind and every activity should be adding value, either directly or indirectly. If it is not, then it should be eliminated, not computerized.

These principles can be embodied in quite simple advice to employees: in the early 1990's staff posters in every building operated by ASDA (the UK superstore operator) proclaimed: *'If you are not helping a customer then you should be helping someone who is'* - simple advice which makes an important point.

From an information systems perspective the internal value chain is a valuable way of identifying where better information and systems are needed, especially to show where integration through systems could provide potential advantage over competitors (or reduce current disadvantages). This may have to be accompanied by new organizational structures to reflect the better way of operating and managing related activities. A logical approach to identifying how IS can improve the business is:

1. Improving relationships with customers and suppliers in all aspects of their interface with the organization (e.g. integrated customer information).

2. Improving the critical information flows through the primary activities, namely removing bottlenecks and delays, ensuring the accuracy and consistency of information used (e.g. total stock management, customer service monitoring).

3. Improving the systems within each primary activity to achieve local improvements in efficiency etc. (e.g. warehouse control, fleet management).

4. Improving the way support activity-based systems can best assist the primary activity management as well as meet central requirements (e.g. budgetary control, personnel data).

5. Improving the efficiency within the support activities by local systems development (e.g. financial consolidation, asset registers).

This may sound perfectly logical - it is driven from the outside and it deals with the critical parts of the business before the non-critical - but it is almost the reverse of the approach that has been taken over the last thirty years. The result is that small armies of people (often 10-20 per cent of all the 'white collar' people employed) sit at the boundaries between business activities and systems operations, reconciling information and analyzing the differences between the two, all day long!

There is scope in most organizations to radically improve these interfaces by using more appropriate information flows and by re-defining the ownership and use of information. This will not only save money, it will improve the ability to add value.

Using value chain analysis will force management to ask searching questions about the strengths and weaknesses of existing systems. It will identify key areas for future investment, especially by the integration of organizational activity. Key aspects of the method of analysis are:

1. It reinforces the business unit approach to assessing business requirements and therefore makes better links to business strategy.

2. It is independent of the current organization structure and clearly separates primary and support activities in terms of criticality of systems needs.

3. It concentrates on why the business is there - to add value to satisfy the customer - and this enables more focused questions to be asked about the activities and systems, such as: How can it be done better, or cheaper, or both? Do we need to do it at all?

By considering the way information flows through and is used by the business, and having regard to the external industry value chain, an organization can identify those parts of the business and its external relationships that can be improved by better information systems.

This is a high level of analysis which helps to avoid irrelevant details and maintains a view of the wider picture. This level of analysis is essential if more detailed techniques are to be used to any benefit. Without the 'big picture', we can be certain that lower level analysis in confined areas of the business will only provide partial solutions, sub-optimization and an ineffective use of analysis time. With the 'big picture' to hand, however, we can direct detailed analysis more effectively and maintain the coherency and completeness of our business models at all levels.

Business process redesign

Partly as an evolution of systems thinking, and partly as a result of the total quality management experience, many progressive businesses have taken up the idea that business processes can be radically redesigned. The argument is that business processes are more an accident of history than conscious planning and there must therefore be significant benefits to be gained.

The depth and scope of change

Depth of change

There are three levels at which we can approach business processes:

- We can simply set about taking stock of business activity generally, because we are not sure who is actually doing what and we need to be able to allocate operational costs on a more informed basis. Should we find that any activities are particularly inefficient or time consuming, we can explore the application of information technology to their improvement.

  This level we can reasonably refer to as *business process improvement*, because we are not trying to redesign or radically change anything. We are just trying to make things work a little better. Most pundits would *exclude* this level from any definition of BPR.

- We can look at the business more carefully, not just to identify activities but the way that they combine into business processes which would be recognized in the outside world (by customers and suppliers, as well as by other business partners such as banks and transportation service providers). In order to gain really significant benefits we decide to look at the bigger picture and go for wholesale change: elimination of redundant activities, redeployment of inventory, close sharing of information with partners. This significantly changes the way the business works, and also the way that our business partners work.

  This is one view of what most people do regard as *business process redesign*. We are looking for the 80% improvement, not just 10% here and there.

- At the most extreme level we can try to find completely new business process models from a clean sheet. This is rarely referred to in the BPR literature but it is increasingly required of businesses to do just this. For example, a public sector organization that is asked to go 'private' needs to ignore all current thinking about process because it will be bureaucratic and wholly inappropriate to the commercial model that they seek. The challenge is to find a new process model from first principles.

  We can refer to this level of approach as *business process invention*, although this is not yet a term that is widely used.

Inevitably any real case will be something of a mixture of these three levels of approach. Some actions will be as simple as automating current operations more efficiently; some will involve redesign of business interfaces for more effective operation, and some will demand completely new thinking.

The question of scope

As well as the degree of change we must decide the scope of change. Are we dealing with one department, with a whole business unit, or with a complete industry? Figure 5.6 shows how we can define the different scope of change at the level of: local redesign, internal redesign, interface redesign and industry network redesign.

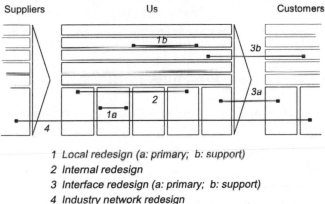

1 Local redesign (a: primary; b: support)
2 Internal redesign
3 Interface redesign (a: primary; b: support)
4 Industry network redesign

Figure 5.6 The nature and scope of BPR

These two ideas can be combined to create a web, within which we can negotiate and position our intentions, as shown in Figure 5.7.

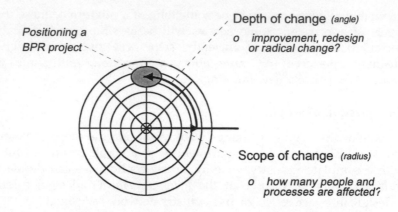

Figure 5.7   A 'web' identifying the scope and depth of BPR

Principles of BPR

The principles of BPR have been established by one expert[4] as follows:

- *Organize around outcomes, not tasks*:   process models out of information analysis let us see more clearly what the outcome is, and how it is derived.

- *Have those who use the output perform the process*:   well designed information systems can integrate the overall process and - in effect - enable the ultimate users of the output to initiate the production of the outputs themselves.

- *Subsume information processing into the real work*:   there is no need to have a separate operation to achieve information processing - technology makes it possible for a workstation to be provided at the point where the real work is done, providing seamless access to all of the information and processing capability that is required.

- *Treat dispersed resources as centralized*:   networking technologies make it trivially simple to locate information workers anywhere, while maintaining central control.

- *Link parallel activities*:   Very often there is duplication of activity; information   analysis   reveals   this   duplication   and   -   by

---

[4]   See 'Re-engineering the Business', Professor Sid L Huff, *Business Quarterly* Winter 1992.

understanding the underlying information structure - makes it possible to eliminate it or reduce it.

- *Put the decision point where the work is performed*: too often work flow is interrupted so that approval can be given by a more senior authority; by making the basis for the decision clear and by making all the requisite information available the decision point can be removed to the point where the real work is being done.

- *Capture information only once, at source*: the level of duplication of information in most organizations is alarming; for example, a national bank had even recently eighteen different places where it kept customers' names and addresses - this can be (and should be) avoided.

The relevance and contribution of information to BPR is quite clear from this statement of principles. The tortuous processes that we find in 'ordinary' businesses derive from the historical difficulty in making information quickly and easily available at any location where it might be needed. This is no longer a problem and becomes the seed for new ideas about how businesses can operate differently.

There is much more to BPR however. It is easy to ignore the consequences as seen by employees and management. For the first time, the role and job security of middle and senior management is being challenged on a wide scale and with obvious consequences. The impact of BPR is wider than just systems, as can be seen in the summary of seven key aspects of BPR in the table below.

Summary of BPR

Some experts are inclined to dismiss the business process re-design approach as being no more than a re-packaging of ideas that have been around for many years. This may be true, but to dismiss it on these grounds is to ignore the fact that it has captured more imaginations and more management energy than many other recent management fads.

Because of its close association with information systems thinking and its reliance on systems in support of change, we can be sure that the general approach to managing business processes will continue to evolve and will be with us for some time.

The table below summarizes the differences between traditional and process-oriented thinking, according to seven aspects of the typical business. The traditional viewpoint is on the left, and the process-oriented viewpoint on the right:[5]

Table 5.1 A comparison of traditional and process-oriented thinking

Traditional orientation	*Aspect*	Process orientation
Internal	*Business focus*	Customer
Hierarchy	*Organization*	Matrix
Diffuse	*Customer contact*	Single point
Control	*Managerial role*	Facilitate
Buffer stocks	*Work in progress*	Just in time
Functional	*Performance measures*	Customer
Internal efficiency	*Information and systems*	External effectiveness

Critical success factor analysis

The approaches described so far have shown how the business can be analyzed to identify how new or better information and systems could improve its performance. However, little account has been taken of what the management want the business to achieve in the short, medium and long term - i.e. the objectives which have been set. By analyzing these specific targets new information and systems needs may arise and can be prioritized.

Definitions and examples

Figure 5.8 shows the key features of critical success factor (CSF) analysis. Before describing how this can be done, the terms involved need some definition:

- *Mission statement*: a broad statement that provides a general framework within which the corporation operates, and which normally expresses the beliefs of the management as well as the long-term aims of the enterprise. For example, in the case of a petroleum company: *'The company is a leading retailer of petroleum products and aims to ensure an equitable distribution of the results of increasing productivity among its shareholders, employees and customers.'*

---

[5]   Based on work by Joe Peppard, Cranfield, 1993

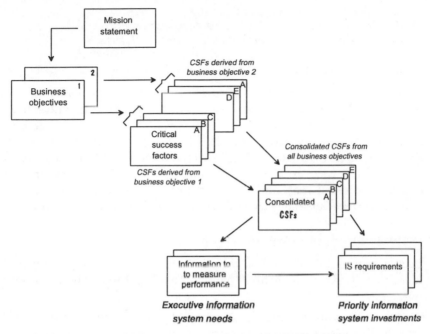

Figure 5.8 Critical success factors in context

- *Objectives*: are specific targets for the business (or function within the business) which are expected to be achieved in a particular time scale. Where possible they should be quantified and must be measurable in some way: they are what the business wants to achieve in a given time scale, normally one to two years, although longer-term objectives can be set. Following through the oil company example some objectives might be:

1   *to achieve 2 per cent improvement in market share;*
2   *to extend outlet coverage in Scotland and Wales to levels elsewhere;*
3   *to increase sales of non-oil products in existing outlets;*
4   *to reduce costs of distribution by 5 per cent.*

- *Critical success factors*: are those things which must go right if the objectives are to be achieved. There should not be too many for each objective otherwise the objective is effectively unachievable. Five to eight CSFs per objective would be normal. Certain CSFs will recur across objectives, thus giving them a heavier weighting in terms of the business dependence on their satisfactory outcome.

A   *effective regional and local pricing;*
B   *increase consumers' brand awareness and loyalty;*
C   *improve non-oil product range to attract customers;*
D   *review all sites in terms of performance and productivity;*
E   *ensure lead free petrol demand is matched by supplies at outlets.*

CSFs must be the product of the management's analysis of the objectives which they have set. There is little point in setting objectives unless some process is undertaken to identify the key actions necessary to achieve them. The CSFs introduce interim targets which are essential steps or preconditions to the achievement of longer-term goals. They help to avoid the situation where at the year end objectives are not met, and the need to have an inquisition into the reasons why because they provide a basis for shorter-term control.

Implications for information systems

Having established the CSFs, then IS actions to deal with them and responsibility for those actions have to be established. These fall into two types:

- All CSFs will require improved information to monitor their achievement, through key performance indicators. If something is critical to success then top management will require regular feedback on progress towards its successful achievement. We therefore establish the need for an executive information system (EIS) which makes this information available and may also provide new methods of information capture and analysis. The EIS itself is just another IS investment, of course.

- Many CSFs may also require systems enhancements or stimulate new thinking about completely new systems. For instance, given CSF 'C' above, it is quite likely that sales of non-oil products are not recorded and analyzed in a consistent way, if at all, and therefore a new system will be needed. The need for such systems improvements may have come about through other analysis routes or merely intuitive creative thinking; ultimately CSFs are a valuable way of assessing their relative importance in the light of the business objectives, as well as a stimulant to new thinking.

Once defined, CSFs may be mapped to the activities in the business. Hence - in conjunction with the other techniques - CSFs can help to focus attention on the IS contribution. A high cost activity in the internal value chain which adds considerable value and has many

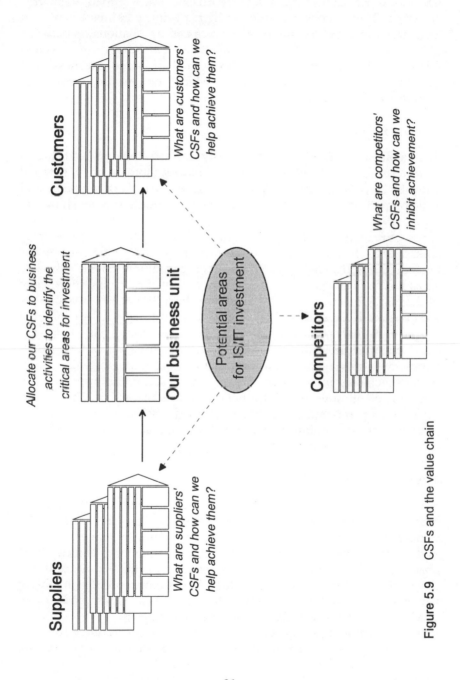

Figure 5.9   CSFs and the value chain

CSFs is more critical than low cost, low value added, CSF free activities. They therefore qualify for higher priority IS investment.

In large organizations there can be a cascading relationship between objectives and CSFs. Corporate objectives will have certain related CSFs, which may in turn be the source of some business unit objectives, which produce CSFs which drive functional and departmental objectives.

A wider focus on CSFs

This analysis technique is essentially inward looking and has a short-term focus. It can be adapted to have a more creative, external value by considering the likely CSFs of major customers, suppliers and key competitors - i.e. other parties in the value chain as shown in Figure 5.9.

The CSF analysis technique is not aimed primarily at IS opportunity assessment - it is a general business strategy tool. However, it has been used extensively by companies and consultants to elicit the key areas for IS/IT investment. It is a way of achieving a consensus view of the management as to where the most beneficial IS/IT investments are to be made. It enables IS/IT potential investments to be evaluated on a non-financial basis, namely by how they will help the achievement of objectives. Hence priorities can be set and resources allocated by management on a more informed strategic basis, not on the IT specialists' preferences. Equally importantly, this approach can help to elicit the key information requirements of the senior management, remembering that it is always better to have a crude measure of something important than an accurate measure of something that does not matter.

The CSF process

Since it is important to achieve consensus throughout, the process must be managed carefully. Before embarking on CSF analysis the mission and objectives must be set by senior management and understood throughout the organization - vague or misunderstood objectives will lead to imprecise, confused success factors. Once this is done, it is best that CSFs are established by a group process involving key managers, rather than separate interviews. This leads more quickly to 'real' business CSFs and earlier agreement.

Once agreement is reached the potential IS opportunities for each CSF should be considered, again in a group brainstorming session, with the help of the IT management. The main risk at this stage is that each option is over-evaluated by the group. It is better to allocate detailed evaluation to someone with a more detailed knowledge so that they can report back later. The CSFs and related IS options and priorities must be understood and endorsed by the senior management team, and then communicated to all those whose actions will affect their achievement.

As the business objectives change over time, so will the CSFs and hence information systems needs and priorities. Therefore it is important that the analysis is revisited regularly by management and that the existing priorities are reconsidered if any of the CSFs change for any reason. This provides management with a way of reviewing the IS/IT strategy from a business perspective and makes their IS/IT decision making more meaningful.

Information analysis

Value chain analysis produces a high level picture of the key external and internal aspects of the business and it can help to identify the need for information investment. Before these areas of need can be addressed a more detailed analysis of information use and information content is needed. This will identify where data originates (inside and outside the business) and who should be responsible for its management and use. It also provides a basis upon which to define

- databases and who should have access to them;
- which processes must be carried out first and which can be carried out in parallel;
- system interdependencies and timing requirements; and
- required changes to organizational responsibilities.

From this more detailed analysis, a logical plan of development can be determined. Each project can be tackled in the most appropriate way (as will be considered later in this book), but within the context of an overall information-based model of the business which shows how the systems will interrelate.

It is important in defining detailed requirements to follow through the rationale of the value chain analysis. The external data required and information relationships with suppliers and customers should be addressed first, followed by the linkages through the primary value chain and its contained activities. Once this stage is thoroughly understood and no key items have been omitted and duplication of tasks or data have been rationalized, then the requirements of each of the main activities can be analyzed within the overall context. It then follows that the support activities should be assessed in terms of the control functions and also the way they can enhance the performance of the primary operations.

The techniques for carrying out such an analysis fall into two main categories: process analysis and entity analysis. The results of such analysis are illustrated in Figure 5.10a (a high level process model for a retailing business) and Figure 5.10b (a high level entity model for the same retailing business).

Process analysis

The first technique looks at business processes and the detailed way in which information and goods are moved through them; this involves an analysis of inputs, the process steps applied to those inputs, and the resulting outputs.

An example

Figure 5.10a shows a high level view of the processes in a retailing business in the form of a value chain, but this time with clearly identified movements of information and goods between the main activities. The thicker lines indicate the movement of goods, and the thinner lines the movement of information. It helps us to see such things as:

1. The different ways in which we deal with direct store deliveries and deliveries to RDCs (regional distribution centres or warehouses).

2. The specific movements of information between primary and supporting activities.

3. The lack of any significant activity after the customer sale has taken place.

4. The three different points at which inventory is held: the warehouse, the goods inwards area and the retail area of the store itself.

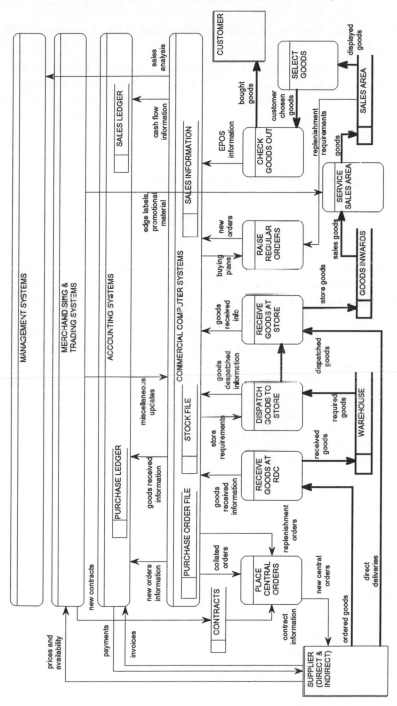

Figure 5.10a   A process model for a retailer

5. The places where we hold key information, such as contracts with suppliers.

It is impossible to show all the detail at this high level but it is possible to agree an overall framework within which more detailed models will be used. The consistency between the high level viewpoint appropriate to management can always be checked against the lower level viewpoint appropriate to operations. In this way the parts of the overall business that are to be computerized can be clearly specified and the boundary between systems and clerical activities can be incorporated into the high and low level models.

Entity analysis

The second analysis technique looks at the way in which information is structured. This is a more abstract level of analysis but it can be used to get behind the current processes and find out *what the business is really all about*, rather than the simpler question of *what it does*; it involves an analysis of the basic building blocks or entities upon which the business is based: 'product', 'employee', 'customer' and 'supplier' are all key entities, about which we must keep information if the business is to able to operate.

Just as the value chain provides us with a generic model of the business process, so we need a generic model of the information that business needs. In the general case there are six areas within which we need information about:

> *the marketplace,*
> *product or service,*
> *procured input,*
> *corporate resource,*
> *corporate performance,* and
> *corporate processes.*

The following paragraphs illustrate the sort of detail which is appropriate to each of these areas.

Marketplace

Information about the marketplace typically includes details of customers, people and organizations that want to have benefit of the product. Also, about competitors and the way that their presence impacts on success.

Specifically, we might expect to have information about: *customers, customer needs, market segmentation, market regions and territories, competitors, suppliers* and even economic political and social factors in some cases.

Product

The material product, service or other 'deliverable' that an enterprise offers to the market; its specification, capability, configuration and operational needs. In the case of service operations, the nature of the service and its speed of response; its information content and the timeliness of the information provided.

Specifically we need product information in terms of: *price, discount arrangements, inventory levels, availability, packaging requirements, product specification, product make-up and bill of materials, product documentation, applicability, function* and *performance specification*.

Procured input

The raw materials and inputs that are required to manufacture or formulate the product or service; their sources and the suppliers offering them. Their characteristics, such as availability, lead time and cost. In the case of service operations, much of the procured input might be external data, taken into the organization and used to deliver service of some kind to the customer.

Some examples in this area include: *procured raw material, components and sub-assemblies, material classification, specification information, sourcing of material and components, compatibility and allowable substitutions*, and *availability*.

Corporate resource

The available standing corporate resource in terms of people, capital equipment and other assets. Also, buildings and property, but not unused inventory (that is better seen as procured input).

For example: *organizational structure, employee information, skills and disciplines, job descriptions, assignment of employees to jobs and tasks, training courses, capital equipment and corporate assets*, and *allocation of capital equipment to jobs and tasks*.

Corporate performance

This is really management information. Probably information about the financial performance of the business and also information about the temporal performance - how quickly and how productively product and service is delivered. Here we would find the raw input to an executive information system.

Typical management information includes: *period results, group profitability, product profitability, corporate performance, average time to ship, volume of production,* and *general accounting information*

Corporate processes

Information about the tasks whereby the operation of an enterprise is sustained: management, financial, administrative and contractual information; information about how sales people are expected to sell, and the procedures whereby a product (or service) is conceived, designed, engineered, manufactured and maintained. Information about any aspect of operations which is perceived by the customer as useful.

Specifically: *sales order processing procedures, purchase ordering procedures, making payments, receiving payments, commercial approval procedures, contract management procedures, cash management procedures, personnel management procedures, corporate management procedures, external commercial procedures, product specification, product development, production engineering, quality control, distribution, installation and commissioning.*

Information about a business process is not the same thing as the process itself. Consider the financial manual in a typical organization, for example. It tells the workforce how it is to deal with financial procedures such as claiming expenses and invoicing customers. The content of the financial manual is information *about* the supporting processes of the business. Equally, an advanced manufacturing planning system includes information about the routeing of work from one point on the factory floor to another, as well as the basic bill of materials.

This idea that we need information about processes is closely connected with quality improvement which is often based on process analysis. Anyone who has been through an ISO 9000 quality management assessment will know what this means: documenting and recording every aspect of how the business works.

However, to someone who is stuck in a business where things 'have always been done this way' the idea will be difficult to understand, because the information about business processes is lost in the heads of the people who have been doing the different jobs - no doubt in the same way for years and years. If we are to change the processes within a business, it behoves us to understand and take stock of information *about* those processes, whether it is written down or simply within the working knowledge of those employed in the business. Until we do this we will never know what we are trying to deal with.

An example

Figure 5.10b shows a high level entity model for a retailing business and illustrates the way in which the results of this kind of analysis are presented.

In using an entity model, one must realize that it simply shows the key things about which we choose to keep information and the relationships between them. For example, Figure 5.10b shows that there is something known as a 'RESPONSIBLE DEPARTMENT' which is accountable for every 'ITEM' that is sold, through something called 'ACCOUNTABILITY'. This tells us that if we have free access to the information used in the business we could call up (on our computer screen) a list of all 'ITEMS' that are sold; we could then pick one, and ask for its 'ACCOUNTABILITY' which would be a reference to the 'DEPARTMENT' or perhaps the individuals who are responsible; we could then ask for the details of that 'DEPARTMENT' including where its 'LOCATION' and what 'CONTRACTS' it has awarded for other 'ITEMS'.

In this way the entity model is no more than a 'navigation' map which tells the reader how it is possible to move from consideration of one aspect of the business to another. When fully developed such a model leads to database designs that ensure that the business will have the detailed data that is needed, and the means to look at it in different ways.

The example in Figure 5.10b leads to a number of observations about the retailing business, having in mind the six different areas mentioned earlier and the need for data in the business:

1. There is no evidence of management information, and therefore it is unlikely that information systems based on this model would provide management with what they need.

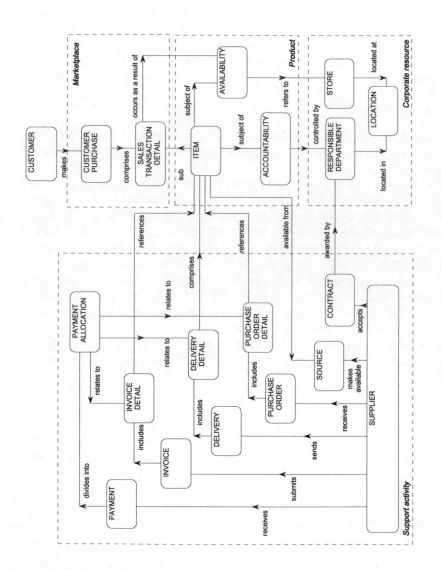

Figure 5.10b An entity model for a retail business

2. There is a good deal of information about supply activities: letting contracts of supply, placing orders, taking delivery, issuing invoices and receiving payments; these activities are all to do with support and there is no evidence of information about customer-side activities.

3. Despite this focus on the supply side, there is no explicit evidence about supplier performance (although it might be 'contained within' the supplier entity, or derived from operational data about orders and deliveries as and when it is needed). We could choose to extend the model to achieve this.

4. There is information about retail stores and the location that they are in, but nothing about employees and the skills and capabilities that they have. In a business that does not care about the contribution that employees make this is appropriate, but if a business wishes to actively manage employees and use information systems in so doing, then the model needs to be extended to include employees and related entities.

5. Most interestingly, the customer is not actually within the scope of the model. This business has no explicit information about customers; it is only be possible to 'see' them through the individual purchases made. It is *not* possible to see the sum of all the purchases made by an individual.

The reader may be aware that many retailers have addressed the problem of customer information by providing machine readable cards which are used to identify customers effortlessly at the time of purchase. These cards can also enable customer account facilities by allowing purchases to be charged upon presentation of the card.

Summary of information analysis

One benefit of information analysis is to find unrealized potential in existing systems and data, in the context of the future business needs. Weaknesses are to be expected but strengths are also sometimes revealed. In one organization a system deemed to be virtually useless was realized to have new potential uses. The problem was that over time the knowledge of what the system did had decayed, and only one person was still using all of its features. By this person re-training the others and developing better user documentation a major re-development was avoided and benefits were achieved very quickly.

These techniques can be used at different levels in the identification and development of systems. While this chapter is concerned primarily with identifying the business advantages of information systems it is worth noting that information analysis is - when properly used - a continuous process which is applied at different stages:

Strategic analysis

- Information analysis can establish the 'information boundaries' of the business and show how they can be extended, so as to extend the influence of the business with its partners.

- Conceptual models such as the value chain can be augmented with the key processes and information movements, so as to begin understanding the operational aspects of new business ideas.

- Entity modelling can be used to avoid the common fixation on business processes and to seek out new ideas for business development which are not constrained by process thinking.

Requirements analysis

- When the formal information systems development process begins, outline process and entity models are used as the basis for much more detailed business modelling with operational management and staff.

- From these, data flow diagrams are developed to specify the detail of business process, and data models specify the detailed content of databases; this then constrains the content of printed reports and enquiry screens.

Informal development of systems

- In the case where development is less formal, tools for the rapid development of systems by end users use the same techniques for building the system.

- Re-usable (or even disposable) computer program code can be generated automatically from a process model, avoiding the delay involved in getting the IS department to do the job.

- A database or a database enquiry can be generated from a data model, so that managers and users can look after their own local data and develop their own enquiries upon centralized corporate data.

Other comments

A danger with this kind of analysis is the enormous volume of information associated with the models when the detail is addressed. It is important that this is not done too soon otherwise the key requirements will be lost in a mass of detail and an equal volume of paper. The use of technology support for information analysis is a popular idea and there are now many software packages available to help in this task, although quality and comprehensiveness varies.

High level models will have a long life but the detailed models need to be maintained. Entity models are particularly enduring and in times of operational change they can offer a unshifting foundation for employees to hang on to. At a time of radical change in a construction company, the deputy managing director issued a memorandum which basically said: *'This is going to be a very difficult time, but don't ever forget that this business is still about **contracts**, **projects**, **plant**, **subcontractors** ....'* and so on. A clear statement of the key entities in the business, if ever there was one.

The final comment on information analysis has to be about documentation. In the final analysis, successful information systems will always depend on our ability to do information analysis and to document our ideas without ambiguity and equivocation. Poor documentation of systems has led to enormous unnecessary costs over the last thirty years. Worse, poor structuring and poor documentation of the business's information resource not only produces high costs but also leads to lost future opportunities.

Summary

As was argued in the previous chapter, the appropriate level at which to establish the IS requirements (or demand) for an organization is the business unit. The framework and tools described in this chapter are used most appropriately to identify the information and systems requirements and opportunities or threats at that level. They provide the means by which management can assess the IS/IT implications of their business situation and strategy. The result is a portfolio of requirements and priorities plus an understanding of the value of existing applications.

No one tool or technique will help in identifying all the requirements and no technique is a substitute for knowledge of the business, or astute creative thinking. However, each of the tools can enable individuals' knowledge to be applied and focused on the role systems can play in business success. By assessing the requirements from a number of viewpoints and with a number of techniques, the most important can be confirmed and the chances of missing important options are reduced. All the techniques can be used by line management and IT specialists in concert; bringing these two communities into useful discussions - perhaps for the first time - is the most immediate contribution that the tools and techniques can make. They each have attributes and characteristics that help to bridge the gap between business and technical thinking, especially the information analysis.

Most organizations consist of more than one business unit. In terms of information systems, the business units are likely to be at different stages of development, but each could no doubt benefit from the exchange of knowledge, and the corporation itself will benefit from finding the most effective and economic means of supply. By using a common framework and applying similar analytical tools, that understanding can be transferred more coherently from one part of the business to another. Where there are clear potential advantages from synergy - where companies trade with one another, deal with similar suppliers and customers, have similar processes or products - then the use of the same rational approach to requirements determination will yield more benefits in relating the business needs. One key feature of the process described is the need to consider what others in the industry are doing, why they are doing it, and any consequent impact. Such knowledge can be transferred from one industry to another; for example, what has happened in the use of EDI in the car industry may have implications for how EDI develops in other manufacturing industries such as domestic appliances.

One last point worth reiterating is that however the plan for systems investments (the demand) is arrived at, it must represent the agreed consensus view of all the senior and functional managers as well as the IT department. If it does not, it will never be implemented successfully. If the plan has been established by a business driven, structured, participative approach as proposed here, that consensus is more likely to be achieved.

Having identified future requirements the next major IS/IT issue is how best to satisfy that demand: the supply strategy. The next chapter considers how the supply alternatives can be considered using a portfolio approach to applications and business needs.

6

Creating an environment for success

Introduction

Chapters 4 and 5 considered the integration of IS/IT strategy with business strategy and establishing the business requirements for information systems. The IS/IT strategy must also resolve how these requirements can be met and how their supply should be managed.

Differences in the requirements lead to a need for different approaches. These must be co-ordinated effectively and they must provide an environment within which all the requirements can be satisfied. As requirements develop and change over time, the approach to supply will also have to evolve. This will affect the development and management of each application, the information resource, and the technology used.

Managing the development of the IS/IT supply environment is the responsibility of business management. The requirements can be considered as a portfolio of IS applications, some of which exist already, some that are required in the short term, and others which are potential developments.

The contents of the portfolio will evolve over time but by dividing applications into different types it is possible for each application in the portfolio, and the portfolio overall, to be managed more easily. It will also maximize the business contribution and optimize the use of available resources. Hence the IS application portfolio is like any other business portfolio (for example: products, customers and investments) and in the same way it enables each application to be understood and managed according to its key characteristics. The most important characteristics are its *current* and *future* business value.

This chapter presents a means of analyzing and applying the IS application portfolio. It shows how it can be used to choose appropriate supply side management strategies, drawing on lessons from managing other business portfolios. These strategies provide a framework for:

- improving the contribution of existing systems,
- allocating resources more effectively, and
- ensuring that the best approach is adopted for new applications.

The portfolio model is not complex but it provides valuable insights and enables management to make more informed and more consistent judgements about IS/IT supply.

Application portfolio analysis

There are many ways of classifying information systems. In the past most have been based on how systems are provided rather than the contribution they make to business success.

There is a classification scheme originally developed by McFarlan which is more helpful.[6] It compares the role of IS/IT between different organizations and enables an organization to analyze its mix of existing, planned and potential systems. It takes the form of a matrix and classifies an application as:

- high potential,
- strategic,
- key operational, or
- support,

according to its current and future contribution as perceived by business management.

---

[6] McFarlan, F.W.; 'Information technology changes the way you compete', *Harvard Business Review*, May-June 1984.

STRATEGIC	HIGH POTENTIAL
Applications which *are critical* to achieving future business strategy	Applications which *may be important* in achieving future business success
KEY OPERATIONAL	SUPPORT
Applications upon which the organization *currently depends* for success	Applications which are *valuable but not critical* to business success

Figure 6.1   The information systems applications portfolio

These terms are defined in Figure 6.1. The matrix can be used by senior management, line managers, users and IS professionals to achieve a consensus view of the contents and implications of the portfolio.

STRATEGIC	HIGH POTENTIAL
EDI with wholesalers and retailers *MRP II* *Market analysis and sales forecasting* *Product profitability analysis* *... etc*	*Expert system for fault diagnosis* *Manpower planning* *Electronic product specification (STEP)* *... etc*
KEY OPERATIONAL	SUPPORT
Bill of materials *Stock control* *Product costing* *Personnel database* *Accounts receivable and payable* *etc*	*Budgeting* *General accounting* *Payroll* *Word processing* *Electronic mail* *... etc*

Figure 6.2   Example portfolio for a manufacturing company (partial)

Figure 6.2 shows a partial portfolio for a manufacturing company. Some systems may already exist, some may be under development and some may just be ideas, but all of them are placed in the matrix according to the current and future contribution that they actually (or potentially) offer. It is important to understand that the positioning of an application may vary from one manufacturing company to another, depending upon corporate maturity and strategic objectives. The strength of the portfolio model is not that it provides a prescription for classification and management approach; rather, it is a vehicle for constructive and informed discussion and agreement.

The strategic analysis tools described in the previous chapter identify new opportunities and ways to realize the untapped potential of existing applications. To follow through, the value of each application must be assessed in more detail. For example an application might:

- have high future potential which is currently under exploited;
- have the potential to be extended or enhanced to be of more value;
- be more valuable if integrated more effectively or used more extensively;
- be critical to the business but suffer from poor quality data;
- need to be redeveloped to meet changed business requirements;
- be transferred to more economical and up-to-date technology;
- provide more facility than is needed, thereby allowing simplification and reduction;
- have no current or future value at all and therefore should be discontinued.

Based on such an assessment of its value a plan can be developed for each existing application.

The portfolio model helps us to see the balance of investment in terms of resources and funds. We can see where effort is currently being deployed and where it is planned. If this does not suit corporate objectives resource can be changed or redeployed. For example, most companies would wish to focus on strategic and key operational applications but it is surprising how often effort is dissipated in the support category. Remedial actions might include reducing the resources used for support systems, buying off-the-shelf packages to service support applications, bringing in outside manpower, or simply a real reduction in overall investment if neither funds nor staff are available.

This portfolio model has many similarities with the product portfolio model usually known as the 'Boston box' (see figure 5.2). Developed by the Boston Consulting Group, this model is useful in deciding how to resource the development of products at different stages in their lifecycle. The same idea applies to information systems applications:

- In the beginning, there is just an idea for an application, which may be championed by only one person: a *high potential* application. The potential for the idea has to be explored and appreciated by the company at large before any substantial investment is made. The idea may be rejected and - should it have actually been implemented - it falls directly to the support category. *High potential applications may be compared to the 'problem children' of the Boston box.*

- When the organization at large has agreed the importance of an idea and decided to act upon it, it becomes a *strategic application*. It is likely to need significant senior management support and it will be important to move quickly. Not only are such applications expensive in resource and investment, the competition may be onto the same idea. *Strategic applications are like 'rising stars'.*

- Applications which have become widely used in an industry are known as *key operational*, because the are critical to the core operations of a business. Increasingly, these kinds of application may be acquired as software packages although they are not cheap and they will usually require a good deal of implementation effort. *Key operational applications are like cash cows; they are critical to the generation of revenue and profit.*

- Applications which are important to just one department (such as a specialized budgeting system), or which are universal in nature (like word processing) are not strategically significant although they are valuable to keep costs down or to keep things under control. *Support applications are somewhat comparable to 'dogs', in that we like to or have to have them around, but they are not critical to current or future success.*

The decision as to where an application fits in the portfolio requires us to understand the main reasons or driving forces which might affect it. Only then can the resulting issues be successfully managed. Some of the key factors are as follows (summarized in Tables 6.1 through 6.4).

High potential applications

The basic philosophy of high potential applications is research and development - controlled experimentation to identify the potential benefits, opportunities and costs involved. Only when this is understood is it possible to decide if further investment is worthwhile and how the next stage of application development should be managed.

For example, in Figure 6.2 the potential electronic product specification idea needs to be evaluated not just by the company but also by those engineering partners on whose co-operation it will depend if any business benefits are to be achieved.

Table 6.1   Characteristics of high potential applications

Driving forces	Requirements
A new business idea or technological opportunity	The rapid evaluation of prototypes, with an ability to reject failures, before they waste resources
An individual initiative in one part of the business, the idea being owned by someone who champions it	To understand the potential of the application in relation to the business strategy and the likely economics of further investment
The objective, which is to demonstrate the value, and then decide whether and how to exploit it for business benefit	To identify the best way to proceed - what to do next, how that should be done and by whom

Strategic applications

The overriding approach to strategic applications is business driven. The ideal IT approach must be constrained by the business imperative; the prime risk is missing a time-dependent business opportunity; perhaps the most critical facet is managing business change. To be considered as strategic, any application must be related clearly to the critical success factors derived from business objectives.

In Figure 6.2 EDI with wholesalers and retailers may well become a competitive weapon, especially if competitors cannot provide similar responses to the same customers. However, the customers' needs will probably change over time and may vary from customer to customer. EDI must be accompanied by business changes if the fullest benefit is to be achieved.

Table 6.2 Characteristics of strategic applications

Driving forces	Requirements
Market requirements and/or competitive pressures, essentially externally driven (perhaps by suppliers or customers)	Rapid development to meet the business objective, and realize the business benefits within the window of opportunity
Business objectives, success factors and management vision of how to achieve them	A flexible solution which can be adapted further to meet changes in the business environment
Obtaining an advantage and then sustaining it by further developments if possible	Links to an associated business initiative or change to sustain the business commitment to the IS/IT development

Key operational applications

This is the traditional IS/IT domain for which tools and methodologies have been developed over the last thirty years. The best IS/IT approaches, derived from years of experience, should not be compromised for business expediency.

In Figure 6.2 a sound product costing system which links to the bill of materials database and inventory management is essential if product profitability analysis is to be carried out. Its integration with existing systems is critical to achieve consistency and accuracy, because it needs the data that is already available in those systems.

Table 6.3 Characteristics of key operational applications

Driving forces	Requirements
Improving the performance of existing activities, in terms of speed, accuracy, effectiveness and economics	High quality (long life) solutions and effective data management, to ensure a degree of stability and reduced costs of change over time
Integrating systems and data to avoid misinformation and duplication of tasks, to minimize the risk of activities being inconsistently or ineffectively performed	Balancing costs with benefits and business risks, to identify the best solution to the business problem
Avoiding a business disadvantage or preventing a business risk from becoming critical	The evaluation of options available to select the most effective, by means of an objective analysis of the feasible alternatives

Support applications

For support applications the economics of the investment will be the main reason for deciding whether to go ahead and the best approach. It is also the area which the most packaged software is available because support applications are often generic, or common to all industries.

In Figure 6.2 the general accounting system might be out of date and inefficient, but since it is not considered critical its redevelopment would be an economic decision. It is likely that a proprietary package would be the most economic way of meeting the needs.

Table 6.4   Characteristics of support applications

Driving forces	Requirements
Improved productivity and efficiency of specific (often localized) existing tasks	Lowest cost, long-term solutions which often lead to package software and even compromising user needs to the solutions available
Legal requirements which have to be met to avoid prosecution	Avoiding obsolescence by evolution at the pace of the IS/IT industry
Most cost effective use of IS/IT funds and resources, to find the most business efficient solution	Objective cost/benefit analysis to reduce financial risk, and ensure the costs of development are easily controlled

Generic IS/IT management strategies

Clearly the issues to be managed in each segment of the matrix are different, as are the risks of failure and the potential benefits. Therefore, different strategies are needed to manage them.

Based on extensive observation of IS/IT management in real organizations Parsons[6] describes six strategies by which organizations link the management of IS/IT to the general business management. His strategies are:

'general frameworks which guide the opportunities for IT which are identified, the IT resources which are developed, the rate at which new technologies are adopted, the level of impact for IT within the firm' ...

---

[6]   Parsons, G. L.; *'Fitting information systems technology to the corporate needs: the linking strategy'*, Teaching note (9-183-176), Harvard Business School, June 1983

> *'the central tendencies which firms use to guide IT within the business'*

and so we can therefore refer to them as 'generic strategies'.

Generic strategies help in the successful management of IS/IT in the long term, provided appropriate strategies are adopted of course. The characteristics and implications of each strategy are described in detail in Table 6.5. The six strategies are as follows:

- Centrally planned,
- Leading edge,
- Free market,
- Monopoly,
- Scarce resource,
- Necessary evil.

The generic strategies are well titled. The very names evoke a basic understanding of the attitudes and behaviour that each is likely to produce.

The generic strategies

Centrally planned:

- IS/IT strategy is totally integrated with corporate strategy through a centralized, senior, dedicated agency.
- Central planning enables a better understanding of competitive opportunities and requirements.
- It allows resources to be deployed optimally and large investments to be undertaken, especially those which span a number of proposed applications.

This strategy is very demanding of senior management time and can therefore be difficult. It can also become removed from the realities of operational business and may inhibit innovation.

Leading edge:

- Leading edge implies an intrinsic acceptance that IT will create competitive advantage and that state-of-the-art technology must be used (relative to current IT use in the particular industry).

Table 6.5 The generic strategies (after Parsons)

	Centrally planned	Leading edge	Free market	Monopoly	Scarce resource
Management rationale	• Central co-ordination of all requirements will produce better decision making	• Technology can create business advantages and risks are worth taking	• Market makes the best decisions and users are responsible for business results • Integration is not critical	• Information is a corporate good and an integrated resource for users to employ	• Information is limited resource and its development must be clearly justified
Organizational requirements	• Knowledgeable, involved senior management • Integrated planning of IS/IT within the business planning process	• Commitment of funds and resources • Innovative IS/IT management • Strong technical skills	• Knowledgeable users • Accountability for IS/IT at business or functional level • Willingness to duplicate effort • Loose IT budget control	• User acceptance of the philosophy • Policies to force through single sourcing • Good forecasting of resource usage	• Tight budgetary control of all IS/IT expenses • Policies for controlling IS/IT and users
Internal IT role	• Provide services to match the business demands by linking closely with business managers	• Push forward boundaries of technology use on all fronts	• Competitive and probably profit centre intended to achieve a return on its resources	• To satisfy users' requirements as they arise but non-directive in terms of the uses of IS/IT	• Make best use of a limited resource by tight cost control of expenses and projects. Justify capital investment projects
Line management and users' role	• Identify the potential of IS/IT to meet business needs at all levels of the organization	• Use the technology and identify the advantages it offers	• Identify, source and control IS/IT developments	• Understand needs and present them to central utility to obtain resources, etc.	• Identify and cost justify projects • Passive unless benefits are identified

- It involves R&D expenditure and some loss of investment, and therefore requires senior management commitment to the concept (but not their close involvement).

This strategy can be expensive and requires adept management to convert entrepreneurial ideas into successful applications. It is a required strategy if technology developments are to be exploited but it will not suit all applications.

Free market:

- This implies that user management knows what is best for the business, including IS/IT, and can therefore assess its own requirements and satisfy them as wished.
- Internal IT services must compete with outside sources and can expect little attention or support from senior management.
- By the same argument, the IT group may bid for work outside the organization and become less committed to internal requirements.

This approach can cause duplication of investment and differential rates of development across the organization, but it will lead to user-driven IS/IT innovation. It is a strategy which produces disjoint systems that are not integrated.

Monopoly:

- IS/IT is provided by a sole source within the organization which must be used in all cases.
- Spare capacity will be needed to respond quickly to all user demands.
- User satisfaction with the centralized services is the main measure of the effectiveness of this approach; the extent of the backlog will also be important.
- The overall expenditure on IS/IT is easy to identify and control.

The monopoly approach can mean innovation is slow and therefore there will be problems responding to competitive needs. However, a well run monopoly will provide a professional service and quality systems.

Scarce resource:

- A budget is set in advance and applications compete for a share of the resource available.

- A very popular strategy which ensures careful management of IT resources by the use of financial controls.

- Investments must be justified in financial terms.

- It is common to focus on return on investment in setting priorities.

IS/IT is here treated a cost centre and the objective is its controlled, well justified use. This is not conducive the exploitation of IS and IT as a business weapon. This strategy does not recognize changes in demand, and priority setting will be a major issue in the planning process.

Necessary evil:

- IS/IT is only deployed to meet legal requirements and for very high return investments.

- IS/IT is used only where no other alternative is available.

This strategy has many disadvantages. It can happen by mistake, through neglect, or because of overzealous scarce resourcing. Unless IS/IT is almost entirely irrelevant to the business the ability to compete effectively will gradually be eroded.

Symptoms are common in many industries. They include high staff turnover and very defensive IT managers who are unable and unwilling to take any risks. Demoralization leads to a lack of capability. Once such a situation exists it is very difficult to deal with: it will usually require significant expenditure and completely new IT management.

Recognizing generic strategies

In practical terms generic strategies have certain key differences, some of which are more obvious than others (see also Table 6.5).

Central planning and monopoly have certain similarities but central planning is essentially a demand management strategy by which the business and IT managers together plan the best route to achieving all the main demands for applications. Monopoly is a supply management strategy - controlling the supply of technology and resources (not funds) to satisfy the evolving user needs. It does not mean that the IT group does all the work, but it retains authority and controls the way users solve problems within the preferred supply strategy. Scarce resourcing is a financial management strategy which requires users and IT to justify investments in financial terms; it is not the wholly negative attitude to IS/IT that necessary evil implies. Free market and leading edge are strategies for innovation: the former led by business demands, the latter driven by technological developments.

Evolution of generic strategies

These strategies can also be seen in an evolutionary sense. In the early days of IS/IT individual departments developed systems independently and the investments were justified by return on investment (ROI). Capital and development costs were offset against estimated savings.

As the level of investment increased resources became centralized to achieve economies of scale, integration and better engineered systems. However, large monopolies became constrictive, backlogs built up and users became frustrated with the limited supply options available.

The availability of personal computers in the early 1980s enabled users to circumvent these constraints and seek their own solutions. Often this caused a major rift between the monopolistic centre and the newly liberated users. At about the same time the high levels of investment and general concern about the benefits of IS and IT caused senior management to force a profit centre approach. The response of many previously inert IS/ IT monopolies was to acquire yet more new technology. As a fuller understanding of strategic IS/IT potential developed central planning evolved to enable proper links to be made with business strategy.

These trends can be seen in the recent history of many companies. After haphazard beginnings computing was often centralized under the main user: the finance department. Scarce resourcing is a natural consequence of financial control of IS/IT. Many organizations still have IS/IT as part of finance. Most major corporations set up monopolistic style IS/IT 'utilities' in the 1960s and 1970s; many were restrictive monopolies and still are. In the late 1970s and early 1980s many companies (such as British Leyland (ISTEL), Imperial Metals (IMI), Debenhams and BTR) evolved to free market strategies, leading ultimately to independent IS/IT companies. This trend has been followed by many others, including local government bodies and health authorities, in the 1980s. As these new IS/IT companies succeeded they developed strategic applications independently and set out to seek their own markets. This led to problems when the applications were sold into companies which were in competition with the original parent.

Major retailers in the 1980s developed central planning strategies to enable major point-of-sale and network investments. Financial service companies have been less successful with attempts to achieve central planning. Banks with a long history of devolved IS/IT strategies have had difficulty in integrating *systems* to support the integration of *products* and *services*. Newer entrants such as the UK building societies (savings and home loans institutions) have been less IS/IT dependent and have a more centralized culture. However, as they expanded their business into estate agency, insurance and banking following deregulation the central planning approach again became strained. This all indicates that once a free market strategy dominates it is very difficult to convert to any other. One solution is to simply start a new business, as the Midland Bank did when it launched FirstDirect in the UK. This very successful telephone-based banking operation operates an integrated personal banking service, 24 hours each day, 365 days a year.

Parsons describes other problems. For instance, a scarce resource strategy will seriously inhibit the development of strategic applications because:

- business strategy is not known or understood by users making requests;
- business strategy is unknown to the (IT) group doing systems work;
- strategic benefits are hard to quantify.

He identifies similar problems in the case of each strategy but, as he points out, historically management has generally adopted only one approach to managing IS/IT. This would imply that only one generic strategy is prevalent but we know that different strategies are actually required at the same time if we are to have a full and balanced portfolio.

Mapping generic strategies to the portfolio model

Parsons examines how each strategy fits onto the applications portfolio in order to identify the best approach in each segment. He concludes that in each case one or two strategies will work best. This allows us to establish appropriate IS/IT management around the portfolio model.

The overlay of 'ideal' generic strategies on the portfolio model is depicted in Figure 6.3.

Note that:

- Central planning (*strategic applications*) is a demand management strategy driven by the business needs whereas monopoly (*key operational applications*) is mainly a supply management approach; both imply centralization of decision making.

- Leading edge (*high potential*) is a demand management approach driven by technology.

- Scarce resource (*support applications*) is a supply management strategy based on limiting the supply of money.

- Free market (*high potential and support applications*) can be both, allowing users to determine demand and decide on the source of supply.

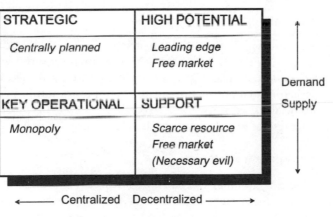

Figure 6.3   Generic strategies related to the portfolio

Given the different driving forces and requirements for the applications in each segment the strategies can be seen to be appropriate. The strategic and high potential segments are about seeking opportunities, identifying future advantages and then managing these new demands successfully. In the key operational and support segments the focus is on resolving current business problems, taking opportunities as they arise, and hence careful management to reduce risk and disadvantage is essential.

High potential application strategies

Over-planning of high potential applications can stifle innovation. The two strategies which will fit best are leading edge and free market, both of which are risky but will cause innovation. Key issues in this segment are concerned with evaluating opportunities and identifying the best way of obtaining the business benefits.

Strategic application strategies

Strategic applications require the central planning approach to ensure the business drive determines the detailed requirement and approach to implementation. It also resolves the level of worthwhile risk to achieve the benefits. Strategic systems will only succeed when they are timely, well specified and closely integrated with the particular business needs.

Key operational application strategies

A monopoly strategy is potentially restrictive but ideal to reduce risks. It provides quality solutions over the long term, a requirement for key operational systems. The highly centralized and controlled approach enables critical issues of functional and data integration to be resolved. This means that all core business needs are met in the most effective way without risk of failure. A very structured approach is essential.

Support application strategies

Scarce resourcing is ideal in controlling support systems investments because it requires a clear statement of the expected outcome before anything happens at all. Equally, the free market can be used allowing users to spend their own funds. Since integration will not normally be a critical issue this can work well. It reduces risk by a steady evolution of the systems ideas, while allowing user discretion and financial control.

Using generic strategies in developing the environment for success

The generic strategies help to develop appropriate IS/IT management in two ways:

Diagnostic

They are a way of assessing the current situation and of understanding and expressing the ways in which IS/IT is currently being managed. There is a strong correlation between the applications developed and the strategies adopted - a cause and effect relationship. The generic strategies can encapsulate the apparent complexity of the existing situation, explain it and describe it succinctly.

Formulative

Once a future portfolio of applications has been identified and the strengths and weaknesses of the existing applications assessed, the generic strategies can be used to identify a migration path. It is possible to avoid the trap of a single universal strategy. It is superficially attractive to say 'central planning is needed', but it is impossible to plan everything centrally. Allowing more freedom, using new technology where needed and tighter, monopolistic control in the critical areas may be more appropriate in the short term. More rigorous scarce resourcing of support systems might yield resources that are urgently needed for strategic systems.

No mixture of diagnostic and formulative use can be prescribed for every situation but the generic strategies provide basic options from which to select. The choice can be made to match the application portfolio requirements. The generic strategies also avoid the need to invent strategy entirely from the ground up - it is easier and safer to modify proven approaches, and then identify the way forwards to implementation.

The application portfolio in a multiple business unit organization

The portfolio model works best at the level of the business unit. Indeed each business unit should assess the IS/IT contribution and management style within their own framework. In a multi-business unit organization this leads to another level of IS/IT management.

For example, consider a diversified conglomerate evolving through acquisition and divestment of business units. The *corporate* IS/IT generic strategy - probably for financial control applications - is likely to consist of a minimal centralized component. Otherwise a free market philosophy can apply to the wider needs of the organization.

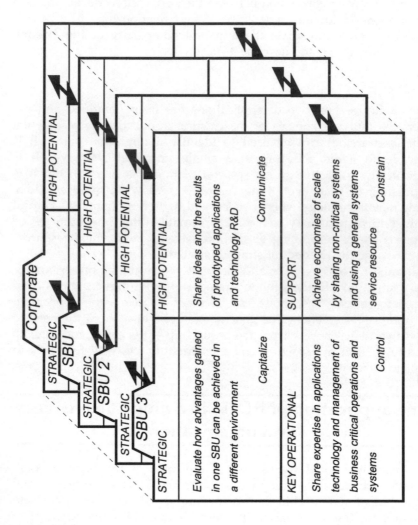

Figure 6.4   Portfolio management across SBUs

However, if the company is predominantly in one industry where synergy is a potential source of advantage this would not work. The business unit strategies must be supplemented by central corporate planning of shared key operational IS/IT applications and a monopolistic control over delivery, in order to avoid proliferation and incompatibility. Equally, where the organization cannot benefit from vertical synergy but consists of like types of companies (such as manufacturing, or retail, or financial services) similar functional requirements will be satisfied more effectively from a monopolistic central utility.

The application portfolio can be applied to each business unit individually and to the corporate headquarters. These analyses will identify unique needs but also similarities of need, and thereby the most economic route to overall fulfilment. For each corporate situation a suitably structured mixture can be arrived at. The portfolio model provides the additional advantage that the analysis of need across business units can be dealt with separately within each of the four categories. Figure 6.4 depicts the gains to be made by a co-ordinated approach across the organization.

In the support box, even if the businesses are diverse, the applications are likely to address similar administrative requirements and packages are a common choice. At worst a limited number of packages should be used, at best a common suite of applications could be used. This will depend on the diversity of the business. Manufacturing and financial services will require different systems, but several types of retail company in different market sectors could easily use common accounting systems, for example.

The same logic applies throughout the matrix but the areas of potential commonality of actual applications are likely to decrease as we progress from support, to key operational, and to strategic. High potential systems have the least synergistic potential but different uses of the same idea may work in different business units.

Even if the businesses are different, providing similar technology in the different business units may enable supply-based expertise to provide better quality key operational solutions for all. Sharing the advantages and experience gained by one unit with another will accelerate the development of strategic applications and help promote an understanding of how to achieve strategic benefits, even if the requirements vary. For example, links to suppliers are likely to offer similar benefits to both manufacturing and retail business units. All this will require a two-level view of the portfolio analysis so that concepts of generic strategies can be extrapolated and shared at both levels - not to drive the strategies but to optimize the strategic effort in each part of the whole.

Issues in managing the application portfolio

The application portfolio matches demand for information systems with the most appropriate means of supply. Applications in the four segments are driven by different issues and need different approaches to their development and management. The role of systems will also evolve over time and they will need to be migrated from one portfolio segment to another:

- From high potential to strategic, as the potential is realized.
- From strategic to key operational as competitive advantage is negated and as disadvantage threatens - the system will also become more stable.
- High potential opportunities may only produce limited support type local benefits.
- Key operational systems can become less critical as the business evolves and may be re-classified as 'support'.
- Finally some applications, mainly support systems, will become obsolete and will need to be removed.

This evolution of systems over time mirrors the evolution of products as seen in the product portfolio. Successful products move over time through a similar life cycle: from 'problem child' via 'rising star' to 'cash cow' to 'dog', before finally being removed from the portfolio. During each stage the product needs to be managed differently, success factors will change and more or less resource will be needed according the shift in its current and future contribution.

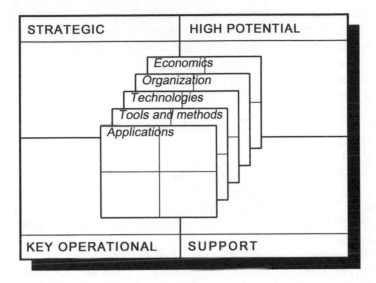

Figure 6.5   Portfolio management - the dimensions of IS/IT

Other lessons can be drawn from the factors bearing upon a product portfolio which parallel pressures on the applications portfolio. This is especially true in a competitive environment, where the systems investments of others can change the potential of our systems just as if they were new products in a changing market.

Figure 6.5 identifies some dimensions of IS development and management which change around the portfolio model.   As an application moves from one segment to another so must the approach to development change. In practice systems have been managed in the same way for years even though their importance to the business has changed. This results in excessive and imbalanced use of resources to achieve ever diminishing benefits. It also means systems progressively fail to meet the changing business needs.

Evaluating IS/IT investments

There is always going to be competition for investment funds, and IS/IT is no exception. The portfolio model provides approaches to justifying these investments which suits the context and the expected benefits of each. Most importantly, it helps us to avoid the trap of the wholly financial justification.

Even better, it can stand as the basis of a clearly understood policy within which proposals can be compared and priorities set so as to maximize benefits and optimize the use of resources.

In all cases the expected costs and resource requirement must be estimated as accurately as possible. This will be easier for support and key operational applications where we understand more easily what we need and how we will provide it. In the case of strategic and high potential applications there will be considerable uncertainty, because we are exploring newer territory.

The estimates should include user costs as well as technical effort and equipment, and they must take a realistic view of long-term costs over the entire anticipated life of the system. Most evaluation processes are conservative and rarely allow for the rapidly reducing costs of IT components. Raw IT costs have been decreasing steadily by some 20-25 per cent per annum over many years, whereas labour and software costs are increasing. All evaluations should be based on real costs not internal transfer prices, even if these are normally used for allocating IS/IT costs to users: they are subject to usage, activity levels and productivity variances and are an unreliable basis for true costing.

Identifying and quantifying the expected benefits of any system can be difficult and they are sometimes only understood after the system is installed. However, it is important to define the target benefits and to express them financially (for key operational and support systems) or in terms of critical success factors achieved (for strategic and high potential systems).

Information economics

In the book 'Information Economics' Parker *et al*[7] assess in detail the ways in which IS benefits accrue and how they can be quantified to help in justifying investments. They consider three main types of application in terms of the benefits expected as follows:

- *Substitutive*: machine power for people power - economics being the main driving force to improve efficiency (this relates mainly to support and key operational systems).

- *Complementary*: improving productivity and employee effectiveness by enabling work to be performed in new ways (this relates primarily to key operational and strategic segments).

---

[7]   Parker M.M., Benson R.J., Trainor H.E.; *'Information Economics'*, Prentice Hall 1988.

- *Innovative*: intended to obtain or sustain competitive edge, for example by changing trading practice or creating new markets (this relates mainly to strategic and high potential applications).

The book then identifies the ways in which applications should be justified and it defines five basic techniques for evaluating benefits: cost benefit analysis, value linking, value acceleration, value restructuring and innovation.

Cost benefit analysis

The traditional cost/benefit analysis, based on cost displacement by a more efficient way of carrying out a task. For example, preparing invoices by computer and transmitting them electronically is more efficient than printing and posting them, both for the sender and receiver.

Value linking

Value linking, which estimates the improvement to business performance by more precise co-ordination of tasks in different areas. For example: being able to invoice customers more accurately by the use of more immediate delivery information; satisfying a greater proportion of customer orders direct from stock by improved use of better stock records.

Value acceleration

Value acceleration, which considers the time dependency of benefits and costs and the benefits of speeding up operations between departments through system improvements. For example: being able to prepare invoices one day earlier or giving sales data to buyers sooner, giving them more time to negotiate with suppliers; improved forecasting information moved more quickly down the supply chain to allow earlier and more accurate production and delivery scheduling.

Value restructuring

Value restructuring, which considers the productivity and improved effectiveness resulting from substantial organizational change, supported by new systems. For example: departments can be combined or even eliminated by means of integrative systems developed across departmental or organizational boundaries;

information intensive tasks such as forecasting, planning and scheduling which can be rationalized and improved at the level of the supply chain rather than within one organization.

Innovation

Innovation through IS/IT can lead to the opportunity of completely new business, which is particularly difficult to value. For example: the value may be in the application itself as in the use of expert systems to diagnose machine faults; alternatively it may be in the image it creates for the company as in the development of home banking services.

Table 6.6 shows how the evaluation techniques align with the portfolio model. The number of asterisks identifies the degree to which the benefit type is likely to fit the application type.

Table 6.6   Types of benefit expected by types of application

	High potential	Strategic	Key operational	Support
Cost benefit analysis	–	*	***	****
Value linking	*	**	****	***
Value acceleration	**	***	***	***
Value restructuring	**	****	**	*
Innovation	****	****	*	–

Number of asterisks indicates degree of relevance

Justifying IS/IT investment using the applications portfolio

Application justification will always lack the precision that we would ideally like, but this is true of any investment decision. The ideas provided by Parker help us to choose the most appropriate approach, especially when taken together with Parson's generic strategies and the portfolio model. Once again, the portfolio categories provide an effective framework to draw these ideas together.

Support applications

The main argument for such systems is improving efficiency, which should be possible to quantify and convert into a financial argument for investment.

If the application development requires the use of scarce (central) resources, it is reasonable to expect potential benefits to be estimated before resources and costs are incurred, to identify the most economic solution within the benefits achievable. If the application is competing with others for the limited resource, then a support application must show a good economic return for the allocation of a scarce resource. If, however, the project can be carried out within the user department's control, then it is reasonable that, since the budget or funding is under local control, the go/no go decision is made by local user management. In this case the IS/IT investment is an alternative use of local funds and is not competing for scarce IS/IT resources from the centre. Hopefully user management will expect the case to be argued in predominantly financial terms. If not, the decision remains their responsibility.

Key operational applications

It should be possible to see all costs and benefits of a new key operational system in financial terms, but this may not allow for all the arguments involved. The most economic solution may not be the most effective. Financial benefits are not the only driving force, and a rigorous feasibility study will be needed to find the best balance of cost, benefit and risk.

The business risks disadvantage if a key operational system falls behind the business needs. For example, it also might be worth spending more to achieve an integrated solution which meets a range of needs more effectively, and upon which new strategic applications can be built; in this case the relationship of the system to others must be included in the evaluation and this will increase the cost. On the other hand it will also increase the intangible benefits which may address critical success factors. This will augment the justification for the added investment through the achievement of business objectives. The reverse argument also applies.

The strategy that works best for key operational systems is monopoly, which implies a central control and vetting of all applications and enhancements. This enables a standard checklist of questions to be considered in the evaluation of any new project. The monopoly approach should also preclude solutions based on only economic expediency rather than total business benefits, although it may mean that a particular application may cost more in the short term.

Strategic applications

Strategic applications are essential to achieving business objectives and strategies. It is important to estimate the cost and benefits as far as possible but the main reasons for proceeding are likely to remain intangible: the critical success factors which the application addresses. This is hardly a case for a detailed discounted cash flow analysis.

The most appropriate generic strategy is central planning. This ensures that IS/IT opportunities are considered and approved in the full light of the business issues and strategies, not as a system in its own right.

Achieving the benefits of strategic applications is partly a question of luck (that the target does not move), partly of judgement (the quality of senior management's business acumen), and partly good management of the application development. The key issues are:

- whether the management team is united in endorsing the project;
- that the organization at large deems the investment worthwhile;
- resourcing the task sufficiently to achieve the objectives in the optimum timescale.

This may need repeated senior management intervention to ensure both user and IS/IT resources are made available.

High potential applications

The very essence of high potential projects is that the benefits are unknown: the objective is to clarify them and assess them. It is the R&D segment of the applications portfolio model and should be justified on the same basis as any other R&D project. Funding should come from a general R&D budget rather than IS/IT central funds: this kind of activity can become a bottomless financial pit if it is not monitored properly. The idea of product champions is appropriate. They can be made responsible for their own projects, given a budget and a brief to deliver results against strictly fixed timescales.

Evaluation is what the high potential segment is really about - nothing should stay in it too long or have too much money spent on it. When initial allocations are used up, further sums have to be rejustified, not just allocated in the vague hope of eventual success. This approach fits the leading edge and free market strategies that the box needs. However, it should be obvious that high potential projects are a main feed to strategic applications; those responsible for strategic applications should be aware of high potential projects and their purpose.

Setting priorities for applications

As mentioned earlier, the mechanisms used to decide whether or not applications go ahead should also be used to set priorities across applications. Some priorities arise from simple dependencies, for instance when Project B cannot proceed before Project A has built the database. Many more are independent of each other and it is important to introduce a consistent, rational approach to priority setting.

Short-term business pressures will change, projects will not proceed as planned, resources will not be available as expected, new opportunities and requirements will emerge. Each of these can change the priorities and we must be able to react intelligently, otherwise short-term issues will prevail. In that short term, resources will be limited and must be used to maximum effect. The main constraint is often the availability of skilled people, in both the user and IT communities.

We have seen that by using the applications portfolio model we have a consistent and appropriate way of assessing the benefits. It also provides a consistent way of prioritizing within each of the four segments. As well as ranking them on similarly expressed benefits, we must optimize the use of resource and deal with risk: the probability that the application may fail to deliver benefits.

Hence, three factors need to be included in the assessment of priorities:

- What it is most important to do: *benefits*.
- What is capable of being done: *resources*.
- What is likely to succeed: *risks*.

Much research has been carried out on why projects fail, and checklists of risk factors are readily available. The main risk factors are concerned with:

- project size and duration,
- business instability,

- organizational rate of change,
- the number of parts of the organization involved, and
- technical factors where new technology is being used.

All applications, wherever they fall in the matrix, should be assessed against such a strategic weighting table to help decide in which segment they belong.

Prioritizing within the portfolio segments

Support

Within the support segment, setting priorities should not be too difficult - those with the greatest economic benefit using the least resources should get the highest priority. This will encourage users to express benefits quantitatively and look for resource efficient solutions, such as packages, to obtain a priority.

Strategic

Within the strategic segment, the basic rationale is equally clear. Those applications which will contribute most to achieving business objectives and use the least resources should go ahead first.

To assess this a simple decision table can be useful in assessing the strategic contribution of different projects, expressing each project in terms of the critical success factors it addresses. This produces a strategic score, or value, for each application. While CSFs cannot be weighted the business objectives can be given relative priorities. Each application definition should clear about how and to what degree it will address critical success factors. Such a decision support tool should not be used mechanistically - a score of 25 is not necessarily better than 24, it simply means the projects are about equally important.

High potential

Like strategic applications, high potential applications should show a relationship to objectives and CSFs, albeit one that is less clear.

Setting objective priorities on scanty evidence is not very reliable, but if an idea potentially impacts many CSFs and clearly stands out it should be elevated above the general scramble for R&D resources. Because it is reliant upon the energy and enthusiasm of its champions, the prioritization and resource used by a high potential application is in effect self-managing, although essential secondary resources can be a problem. The results will depend not only on the value of the idea, but also the force with which it is pursued.

Key operational

Setting priorities for key operational systems is more problematic than for support or strategic systems because the rationale is more complex. The arguments for key operational systems will be basically economic considerations, risk to current business, CSFs and infrastructure improvement. Each of these must be given some form of priority weighting before looking at resource constraints.

In each case the cost and resources used by the project should be matched against its importance in each of the four categories to establish overall priorities.

The question of infrastructure

IT infrastructure is the means whereby systems are developed and operated. It includes the computer equipment, software, networks and people who are all essential to the delivery of systems capability. It also includes common elements of all kinds, such as standards, quality control and project management.

Some applications lead to a direct requirement for new infrastructure. In other cases the sum of several applications makes an infrastructure investment necessary. For example: a new network that will link all offices and provide a vehicle for different applications to be offered at all of those locations, or a new customer database that will service marketing, sales and customer service applications. Infrastructure is important in developing a coherent systems and data architecture, increasing skills, improving the resilience or flexibility of systems and the technology base. This will both avoid excessive costs in supporting the systems and also provide a firm foundation for strategic developments.

We will therefore become involved with evaluating and prioritizing infrastructure projects as well as applications projects. Risk to current business could be assessed in a similar way by asking 'what risks do we run if the infrastructure project does not go ahead?' In general, the priority given to an infrastructure project is inherited from all the applications that it will support or contribute to.

Prioritizing across the portfolio

The remaining task is to set priorities across the segments of the portfolio to decide how much resource to devote to the different types of applications. This is not simple since the rationale for investment in each is different, as shown above. How, for example, can management compare a market analysis system which will help segment the customers more precisely, with a pallet control system for the warehouse which will save two staff?

The approach recommended here can be used to assess all types of applications. The problem is that strategic applications (such as the market analysis system) will score heavily in CSFs, whereas support applications (such as pallet control) will score heavily on economics and key operational systems will score on risk and infrastructure. Management must decide the weighting to be attributed to each type of benefit and then rank the systems.

The relative weighting given to each will depend on a number of business and IS/IT factors such as the following:

- The strength or weakness of the business position will affect the need to defend the current position or to become more innovative.

- The strengths and weaknesses of existing systems and the capabilities of the IS/IT resource, based on previous delivery performance.

- The experience and competence of users in defining requirements and implementing systems successfully.

Another important factor will be the degree of confidence that management has in its own business judgement relative to the need to be reassured by figures. The more confidence that management has in the whole organization's ability to develop effective systems and the more mature is the approach to strategic planning, the greater will be the weighting placed on CSFs relative to financial arguments. It also tends to depend on the strength of the company within its industry, of course.

If the overall plan is developed and maintained in a priority sequence that reflects the following ratio:

$$\frac{\text{Benefits to be achieved (adjusted for risk)}}{\text{Limiting resource consumed}}$$

then it helps both in short- and long-term planning decisions. This is because:

- resources can be allocated where necessary from lower to higher priority applications on a rational basis, with the agreement of users, and

- appropriate resourcing levels for the future can be set, and action taken to obtain the right type of resources to meet the demands.

It is important to communicate the resulting plan to all involved to help them understand the reasons for the ranking of any particular project. Mystery or uncertainty are far more destructive of strategies than the discussion and reconciliation of real problems.

Again the above arguments may lack the precision ideally required for setting priorities, but given that rules for the various factors involved can be established sensibly, it is better than each priority decision being made on a different set of criteria.

In both the evaluation of projects and setting priorities it is important to do some retrospective analysis of results, 'after the event'. A review (but not a witch hunt) must be carried out on sufficient projects to determine whether management policies and strategies are working. It is also important to find out whether or not the expected benefits were achieved. A factor which differentiates successful from less successful companies in their deployment of IS/ IT is management's resolve to evaluate IS/IT investments before *and* after they occurred. Without a review after the event there is no point in having any system of investment evaluation and priority setting.

Summary

Creating an appropriate environment to enable the successful deployment of IS/IT requires three aspects of management to be brought together:

1. There should be a means of ensuring that the strategy reflects the business strategy.

2. The demand for different applications should reflect the real, critical business need.

3. The supply of systems and technology must be appropriate to both the aggregate and particular needs of applications and should be co-ordinated effectively across the whole portfolio.

This chapter has dealt with the third issue by using a matrix model of the portfolio. It has shown how this model resolves many of the key supply issues.

Supply can be managed according to the expected contribution to the business of the different types of IS/IT investments. The application portfolio together with the generic strategies establishes both the overall approach and the best approach in any particular situation. The portfolio model can be easily appreciated by users, senior managers and IS/IT professionals and it helps to reconcile their differing views.

Having established the framework, the management issues involved in the development of applications and supporting technologies can be resolved in an equally effective way, as will be seen in the next two chapters.

7

Managing information systems development

Introduction

The development and delivery of information systems is a challenging process. In the past there have been great difficulties with the process and all that surrounds it. Some organizations have spent many years developing their corporate competence in systems development but others still fail to produce viable systems which are fit for their purpose. There are too many examples of systems which are too expensive, ineffective, or just inappropriate to the business requirement. Business has also learned that the demands made by strategic systems development can be overwhelming.

What we have learned about systems development generally parallels what we already know about the achievement of large and complex projects in other areas of endeavour such as construction and process engineering. In systems development we are faced with the need to specify requirements in an explicit way and to break down complex activities into tasks which we can understand and monitor. We need to develop ways of estimating costs and schedules for systems development work which will reduce the chance of overspending or overrunning. Above all, we need to be able to manage multidisciplinary teams of people who may never have worked together before and who may have difficulty understanding each other's point of view.

The construction industry provides examples which can help us to organize our ideas about systems development. Most of us have seen a house being built and are aware of what can go wrong - for instance, the intending house owner who interferes needlessly with the building work and creates total confusion; the plumber who ruins the work of the plasterer; or the painter who only half finishes his work. In developing information systems we share many of these kinds of difficulty, but the problems are compounded by the abstract nature of the information system as a product.

The house is something which we can easily visualize and quickly sketch on paper, but what exactly is a quick sketch of an *information system* going to look like? The hardware - whether a personal computer or multimillion pound mainframe - can be visualized easily, but it is just a small part of the total system. The part which so often has to be developed every time is the software - the intangible and invisible collation of instructions to the computer which tells it how to work. These computer program instructions are the smallest building blocks of a computer system, but how do they relate to the familiar parts of a house: bricks, slates, timber and internal fittings? A quantity survey of a house is relatively easy to achieve. However, a simple count of the number of 'components' in a computer system is notoriously difficult to estimate - indeed, it is even difficult to agree on what the basic components of an information system actually are.

As well as the problem of conceptualization and visualization there are technical problems. For example, problems caused by the rate of change in the technology that is used to develop computer systems. It is not only the user who is bewildered by ever more sophisticated and powerful hardware and software - every year there are new tools and techniques for the technicians which, even if they are seized upon with great enthusiasm, tend to undermine the users' capability to develop systems.

Other problems relate to the organizational changes that are taking place. Centralized systems development is giving way to devolved authority and capability at the operating level of many larger organizations. These changes may be seen as progress, but nevertheless they present a considerable challenge to all those involved by further undermining the simple ability to learn from experience.

The best approach to resolve these difficulties is the same that we would adopt for any complex project: we need to break the problem down into manageable parts. The detail and nature of the result will be very different, of course. Some of the consequences of these differences are discussed later.

Basic systems development

It is common to use analogies to describe the information systems development task, and here we have already used the example of house building. All analogies have their limits, and it should be apparent already that the nature of an information system, as an end product, is radically different to a tangible physical product such as a new house. The systems development process is concerned more with ideas and abstract models, and it therefore suffers greatly from our inability to visualize and design systems in any simple way. A *completed* information system is no more than machine-readable computer files on a disk or tape. The cost of reproduction of such a finished system is trivially small, whereas the unit cost of building identical houses will never reduce significantly. The proportion of cost in the design of a system is high, whereas the cost of house design is low. These differences are important and affect the economics of the systems industry relative to more traditional industries.

Consider the simple matter of changes. If we decide to alter the plumbing in a house there is much visual evidence that the new pipe work has been done, for example, bright copper around the new joints, paint which has been scraped off the old pipes, and possibly drops of plumber's solder and copper filings on the floor. Who can tell when the instructions in a computer program have been changed? A programmer can make sweeping changes to great volumes of program code in a matter of minutes and there is no evidence at all that this has been done - unless the programmer chooses to leave a comment behind within the program source code. The problems of auditing this type of work, where there is not a shred of evidence that changes have been made, can be insuperable.

We try to deal with these problems by using models to represent our ideas about systems, by putting much emphasis upon the documentation which accompanies the technical work, and by breaking down the work into sensible tasks. We must provide an environment where effective communication between team members is possible. Also, when the pressure is on, we must make more time for review and discussion, not less.

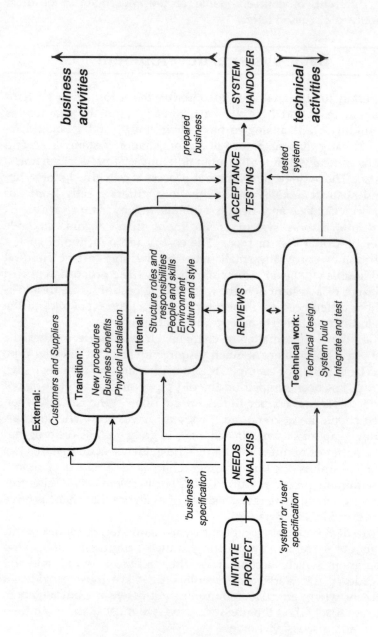

Figure 7.1 Business and technical activity in systems development

Figure 7.1 shows a simple model for the development process where the area of each activity is intended roughly to indicate the effort involved in each of the various activities. As well as the basic tasks it shows the joint involvement in the early and late stages. It shows business activity in the upper part of the diagram and technical activity in the lower half. During a project there will be a great deal for the users to do and we will see that this is often critical to the success of the project. For too long the technical content of projects has been seen to be predominant but this is changing as we affect the business more and more significantly by the introduction of new computer systems. There will need to be new organizational arrangements, new office procedures, and staff training to help them in adapting to the new system and its accompanying technology. In some cases the users will undertake the whole job themselves by using easy development tools and prototyping methods.

The critical stages in any project are the areas of joint activity, especially project initiation and analysis (when the requirement is being investigated), and acceptance testing and handover (when the system is being proved for its suitability and completeness). Any short cuts here will almost certainly guarantee difficulty, delay and additional costs later on, whether during the development process or after the system has been in use for some time.

Most important, perhaps, is the management of the development process. It is evident in practice that the most successful projects are often managed directly by the users. Even where the user management has little competence in information systems and technology, the very act of assuming responsibility for a project (and then demanding clear explanations from the technical staff of what they are doing) can make all the difference between success and failure.

This chapter will first take a traditional view of the basic systems development process, concentrating on the technical activity represented in the lower part of the diagram. Later in this chapter special attention is paid to the analysis stage, where the users' involvement and understanding of the development process is very important.

Getting started: different viewpoints

Figure 7.1 provides a model for the technical and business activities in a project. The detail that lies behind this model will be dealt with later.

As well as the tasks in hand we must understand the different roles which must be enacted. Everyone involved with systems development must understand their role and recognize that other peoples' perspectives on the development process (and what it produces) will be different. We should not expect that each person understands the others' viewpoints in a detailed way, but just to recognize the common ground - especially the benefits that the business expects, the timescales involved and the implementation plan. With this in common then the participants might be more tolerant of the legitimate differences between them.

The house building analogy is useful again here. In building a house most of us would agree that there are at least four key roles to be fulfilled, as follows:

1. The *house buyer* who wants the benefit of being able to live in the new house (compare with the user of a new computer system).

2. The *architect* who has the skill to help the purchaser articulate detailed needs and approve the plans (equivalent to the systems analyst).

3. The *craftsman* who has the physical skills to put the house together from raw materials, according to the construction plans (in the same way that programmers put a computer system together).

4. The *site foreman* who has the patience and persistence to see the whole thing through (just like any good project manager).

It is of course possible for one person to adopt a number of these roles at once. The architect might also be the purchaser, the purchaser might choose to be both the architect and to oversee the onsite work, or the craftsman might be left to undertake the outline design without the help of a professional architect. This is the same with information systems where it is quite common for users to undertake some development of local or personal systems, and where they might assume responsibility for project management. Systems analysts are often expected to write the programs.

There are other supporting roles in both cases, of course. There is the builder's merchant who supplies the materials, the building

Susan - the newly appointed IS quality manager - felt extremely depressed as she sat down at her desk again after the crisis meeting. The original estimating computerization project was where the trouble had all started. It had been started 'unofficially' by the estimating engineers themselves, but since was taken over by the IS department (ISD) - a part of corporate Management Services. Susan let her thoughts run over the different characters who had attended the meeting.

Robert *(chief estimator)* is probably one of the most experienced people around *(Susan thought to herself)*. He's one of those steady people who has worked for the company for years. In the meeting he was very specific about what he needed from the system. He just wanted it to be an estimating system: he wanted it installed in the estimating office for the estimators - for no one else. He presumes that the ISD approach will deal with the current project problems but doesn't want to be personally involved. His greatest concern is to re-organize the detailed procedures in the office (in anticipation of the new system) and to get some of the jobs re-graded through the grading committee. What's more worrying is his unwillingness to get involved with the user requirements specification. His people were generally unwilling to make time for the computerization project and he was applying no pressure to do so. Parts of the new estimating system seem to be really difficult to specify.

Tony Bannister *(systems analyst)* is a relatively new member of ISD and came with a really good career record. Although he has never worked in the process engineering industry he really knows his stuff. His background is programming and systems design and doing the spec for this estimating system ought to be well within his capability. He even has a lot of recent experience in LSDM - the chosen systems analysis methodology used in ISD. His entity models seem to be really well worked out and he is one of the few people around who seems to understand entity life history analysis. What a pity that he doesn't seem to be able to get through to the estimators. When he tabled some of his new specification material you could just see the rest of the meeting trying to pretend they were not there.

Phil Gordon *(senior programmer and designer)* has been in the company for a long time, but always in ISD. He should know his way around. But when he said anything at all at the meeting he was practically ignored. Obviously he is really worried about the database performance and wanted to try and optimize some of the data structures, but no one would discuss it. He even had some ideas for using Windows APIs *(application program interfaces)* and embedded objects to link the user's spreadsheets with the new system.

Harry *(project manager)* has responsibility for the project as the nominated ISD project manager. He's very pressed for resources and loses people as fast as he can recruit them. He's never available to chat things over between meetings. During the crisis meeting he laboured the point that every time the users changed their minds it cost whole days to backtrack and put the specification together all over again. And then he had complained to the users about their lack of interest in project reviews. Robert Frost said he had heard from his people that the review effort was a totally unproductive waste of their time.

Susan thought wearily that there must be some way to get these people together. Robert, Tony, Phil and Harry were undoubtedly the key players and if she could get them pointed in the same direction then there would be a chance for the project to get going again.

inspector who checks the work against the regulations and the banker who lends the money. Similar roles exist in systems development: the software and hardware suppliers, the budget holder, and so on. As indicated above, the four key roles are the user (purchaser), the analyst (architect), the specialist systems developer (craftsman) and the project manager (site foreman). The illustration based upon a meeting about a project in an engineering company gives us an example of the difference in viewpoint (see the box).

User

Users are those who want to have the benefit of the use of the completed system. They must be satisfied at the earliest possible stage that the system will provide the expected benefits, and they must see evidence of progress from time to time while the system is being developed. The extent to which they are involved in the central stages of development varies.

Clearly in the example Robert (the chief estimator) thinks he understands what the benefits will be but he has made little effort to share his hopes with the rest of the project team. Nor is he encouraging his staff to do so. If we dig below the surface we will find that he has lost confidence in the project and expects someone else to sort things out.

The world of the end user is one of departments and employees, of business objectives and critical success factors. The user will have a good understanding of the business but it may be instinctive. The various business functions, processes, activities and tasks may be so obvious to the user that he or she never thinks to explain them to the system developers. The user will see the facilities of the system as business transactions, access to information, reports and analyses, and other primary documents such as invoices and statements of account. The expected benefits can vary widely as we have seen in previous chapters.

Business/systems analyst

The systems analyst is often referred to nowadays as a business analyst, whose overall responsibility it is to describe and document the business requirement in a way the user can understand and which will provide a basis for technical development work.

Tony seems to have all the right skills but he is missing something which will allow the users to relate to him and to join wholeheartedly in his work. It could be that he has no credibility because he comes from the wrong industry, or it could be that his approach is too overbearing.

The world of the analyst is a subtle and demanding one. An analyst must be both creative and receptive - he or she must listen uncritically while the user explains problems, and then help the move towards the new system by explaining options and the implications implicit within them. Analysts must have good communications skills and have the patience to record all that is being said, and later to prepare and present systems proposals which are complete, coherent, and comprehensible to all parties (including the systems developers as well as the end users). This means taking the informal vocabulary and notation adopted by the user and rephrasing the ideas more formally (just as the architect has to make a rough sketch and then formalize it using standard diagrammatic forms and symbols). The analyst will then prepare an outline project plan showing approximate costs and timescales.

This is a demanding, complex and sometimes chaotic process out of which the analyst must draw order and meaning. Business analysis at this level requires the use of models to illustrate and communicate ideas. These are necessarily abstract representations of what is required, and a *logical* rather than a *physical* view of what might fulfil the need: business processes, not computer programs; logical data structures, not physical databases reports and forms; abstract entities rather than real people and real things.

Specialist systems developer

The specialist systems development role has been complicated by the rapid evolution of systems development technology. Where once the computer programmer might reasonably have done all of the technical work this is now less likely. The responsibilities of specialist systems developers relate to the development environment: the computer language systems, operating systems, telecommunications features and database software. It is a complex world where no single person can or ever will be able to understand everything. Just as users and technical people can have difficulty communicating so can the different technical disciplines.

Phil (in our short example) is probably a really nice guy, but is also stuck in the information technology rut. In the face of any problem his answer is likely to be more technology. Yesterday's lessons about technologies that do not work have no effect upon his optimism about tomorrow's newer gizmos.

The world of computer programmers and specialists is a mysterious one to most of us. They must understand the technology, what its limits are, how powerful it is, what it will and will not do, and what dangers and risks it presents. When technology fails they must understand why and (one hopes) what to do about it.

Project manager

It is inevitable that the three disparate roles of user, analyst and specialist need a fourth to hold the whole act together. In the same way that a good foreman will see that houses are built to a proper standard, and that the craftsman understands at least most of what the architect wanted, the project manager holds together the systems development project without actually doing any of the real work. The project manager must have an instinct for problems, the confidence to take decisions and the presence to keep everyone involved on the job productively at work.

Harry seems to have hit his limits. A project manager who is not available 'on call' is going to be no help to anyone on a day-to-day basis, and problems need to be dealt with as soon as they arise. At the same time, he is losing staff - a sure indication that not even the team members are getting his attention.

The world of the project manager is one of lists of things to do, of schedules and of resource management. Everyone on the project must have something to do, it must all be meaningful, and it must be executed in the right sequence. Checks and controls must be put in place and exercised, progress reports must be written so that other interested parties know what is going on, and the project manager has to try to speak everybody's language and to translate as well as arbitrate between the other roles. Except for the intangible nature of the ultimate work product, the project manager in systems development is faced with a very similar task to any other project manager.

Shared interests: finding the critical project success factors

Keeping the different viewpoints in line with each other is one of the keys to success. By working to remind all participants of the higher level issues the project manager can establish common ground which links the technical, organizational and implementation issues.

- The business people must be able to see 'their business' clearly reflected in the work done by the systems analyst. An analyst who changes terms and words needlessly will alienate the users. The 'baseline' that is the current business must always be evident and must stand as a reference point when proposing improvements and changes. Both the analyst and the users must share an enthusiasm for improvement and a clear understanding of the intended benefits of new systems.

- The analyst must also share something with the technical specialists: for example, the way in which the business needs map into the physical components of the finished system. Each 'logical' process must lead to input and enquiry screens which the technical people then specify and construct, and each logical data file must be incorporated into the design for the physical database.

- The project manager has to keep an eye on everything. The detailed project plan cannot be finalized until the initial analysis work is complete and the project manager must take this analysis work on board, understand it, and use it to shape the rest of the project. After all, until the analysis work is done, the project manager has no real framework within which to manage. Once this is in place, however, he or she needs to be very clear with the technical people about the tasks which they are asked to do, hence the importance of the work breakdown structure and the need to relate all technical work to specified elements in the user requirements specification.

- In dealing with user management the project manager needs to maintain their level of commitment. This requires that they are involved in the planning process and that their tasks are fully incorporated into the project plan. Too many projects move slowly but resolutely to the point where the user cries 'enough, I'm just trying to run a business - just tell me when it's all finished'. This is less likely to happen when it is the users' project *and* the users' project plan.

Within each area of specialization there is a great deal of detail of concern to only the specialists. Across the boundaries, where there is shared substance to the project, mutual understanding becomes critical to the success and integrity of the work being done and the system being produced.

Once installed, the new systems and the technology which supports them can still take up a lot of management time. The overall capacity of the hardware needs to be maintained by anticipating changes in business activity and translating that into systems capacity requirements; systems support and enhancement capability has to be provided and internal technology standards and quality control in systems development have to be monitored. Much of this may fall to a technical support group, or there may be a computer operations group which deals with much of this. The time of actual installation is especially critical. As soon as systems come into use there will be a rush of queries from the users, newly discovered bugs and problems to be fixed, and a whole series of concerns about the changes to the business itself.

We have looked at the key areas of systems development, namely:

- the business itself,

- the business modelling and systems analysis work,

- the technical development work, and

- project management.

We have explored the way different people view the developing system, but what are the jobs they have to do?

The main project activities

The main categories of activity are concerned with the business issues and the technical systems development process.

Business activity

Although it is almost traditional to assume that an information systems project is based on analysis, design and programming it is the business activity that ensures real success, and which is increasingly recognised as the more critical portion of the whole.

The intended benefits of a new application vary from simple cost reduction (when there may be little change to organizational arrangements and working practice) to radical business process redesign (when the systems issues fade into insignificance when compared to the degree of business change involved). The relative importance of the business activity in the project therefore also changes. It is not possible to be prescriptive about the planning of the business elements of a project, but there are some general requirements within the organization, outside it, and during the transitional phase.

Internal

Within the organization it ought to be relatively easy to communicate changes and to organize the new operational environment. It is therefore surprising that is so often done badly. One of the factors affecting the way it is done is the dynamic of the typical project: the temptation to leave the 'simple' things to the end in order to address the really difficult parts first is over-riding. This usually means the technical work gets done first and the people are left until it is too late. Unfortunately, it is the people issues that are more difficult to deal with as our systems become more strategic.

Internal issues include changes to physical accommodation, preparing training courses, redefining job descriptions and organizational structure, and (in extreme cases) undertaking to change the culture and attitude within an organization. Consider for example the case where information systems are being used to underpin a new customer-service initiative, whereby all staff are expected to be able to deal with customer queries and satisfy them.

External

More and more systems are conceived at a level above that of the single organization. New technologies such as electronic data interchange (EDI) and more widely accepted standards make it easier to interconnect the systems in different companies.

In this situation the whole process of implementation can slow down markedly. Convening a meeting within the company is bad enough; convening a meeting of representatives from several different companies and persuading them to take joint action can take years. Worse, recent history shows us that such initiatives sometimes fail to achieve anything. When they do succeed the rewards are great. Major retailers around the world have used EDI to exercise tighter control over their suppliers and have markedly reduced operational costs. In the defence industry in the US (and now all over the Western world) an initiative to computerize all aspects of military equipment supply has set new expectations and brought very large numbers of people together in an attempt to unify and integrate their systems. This does not happen easily and it will be decades before the full benefits are seen.

These co-operative initiatives can be achieved through standards development in open committees, as is the case with the international EDIFACT standards for EDI. Alternatively, they can be achieved in a more competitive way in smaller, tighter partnerships. The automotive industry is an example where the main manufacturers have led in the development of joint engineering design systems in order to reduce the time to market for new models and to simplify the detailed processes of design.

These external factors are beginning to affect all major information systems projects and building them into a project plan can significantly extend timescales and increase the cost of project work.

Transitional

Another facet of the business effort required is associated with the transition from the old to the new system. It is easy to analyse an existing system; it is only slightly less easy to specify a new system; however, achieving a successful migration from one to the other requires an exceptional effort which can seriously undermine the chance of success if it is not understood and managed well.

It may be required to run the old and the new systems together for a time, to make sure that the same results are consistently produced by both. This doubles the demands on staff time and it happens at a time when staff will expect to be being trained. Training can take place too early or it could be too late; doing it at the same time as the final stages of implementation is ideal but it is the time of greatest strain. In other circumstances the only viable way to cut over to the new system is - literally - to switch off the old system on a Friday and to go live with the new one on the Monday following. This requires meticulous planning and rehearsal if disaster is to be avoided.

It follows that during the transition a special investment may be necessary to bring in extra staff and to cover overtime costs. The more strategic an application is, the more important it is to get through the transition quickly. Under-investing at this stage will threaten not only the completion of the project that is delivering it, but also the achievement of the intended competitive advantage.

A basic model for technical work

In the general case the essential technical activities are as indicated in Figure 7.2. This is a widely-used model for systems development which identifies seven stages in the work, and the outputs that result from each. The term usually used to refer to these outputs is 'deliverables': they are the material evidence that work has been done. They are principally documents and specifications in the early stages and working programs in the later stages. They represent the only practical basis for agreement, approval and quality assurance; each also represents a baseline for further work in the succeeding stages.

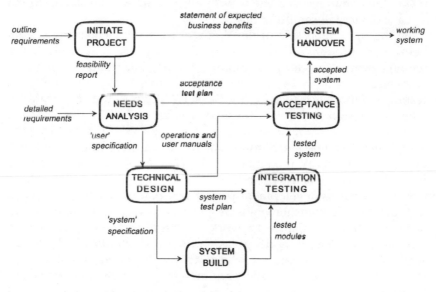

Figure 7.2   A traditional model for systems development

Consider, for example, the required content of the three main deliverables shown at the left-hand side of the V model. The *feasibility report* provides a broad overview of the departments and jobs which will be affected, the business function which will connect with (or be subsumed into) the new system, and any constraints that have to be recognized by the project team. The feasibility report will be itself be constrained by the overall information systems strategy. It will include commercial and financial analyses demonstrating the technical, operational and economic feasibility of the proposal, and it will document the expected benefits.

The *user specification* provides the detail which clarifies the specific business tasks affected by the new system, and the data that is to be to be employed within it. An important feature of the user specification is to define the man-machine boundary so that the interchange between the system and the real business can be clearly understood and agreed. The fine detail within the new system need only be specified in outline.

The *system specification* concerns technical details rather than the real world of the business and the user. It must deal with the way in which the system is to be implemented, the computer hardware resources required, the structure of the programs and subroutines inside the computer, and the way in which data will be stored on the storage devices in computer files.

On the right-hand side of the V model we see the emerging system being put through different stages of testing and ultimately being handed over. The detail of module testing, integration testing and acceptance testing is beyond the scope of this book, but acceptance testing is importance because it is the stage at which the user begins to take responsibility for the finished system and it is the last real opportunity to raise queries and change requests. In particular, the *acceptance test plans* are important for the user to understand and agree. Finally, the V model shows the *completed working system* as natural conclusion of the project.

Any non-trivial development project will require a staged approach in order to give management a proper degree of control, and to give technical staff the chance to work on large complex systems in a modular way. The V model gives a framework within which we can establish the detailed project plan within well understood stages. It shows clearly the close relationship between the early and late stages (analysis and acceptance testing) and the central stages (design and systems testing). The four levels of the model and the progression from the top left-hand corner down to the lower centre and then up to the top right-hand corner reinforces the idea that development takes place at different levels. It is the test plans which establish the horizontal connections in practice, acceptance test plans at the higher level and systems test plans at the middle level. The differences are very important and help to resolve the problems arising from the different viewpoints of the user, the analyst and the technical specialist.

The V model is a useful starting point for a general discussion of systems development. In any particular case where a project is being planned it can be used to define the required deliverables and the detailed approach to the generic tasks of analysis, design, system build and testing. It can be manipulated to show the different approaches to application development which best suit the portfolio model, such as prototyping and other variations on the basic theme.

The main project activities

In a software house, or in the information services department of a large organization, it is normal to find that there is a well specified process for systems development. The stages will be detailed down to task level, the form of the deliverables that are to be produced will be very clearly stated, and perhaps there will be a policy statement on what level of authority is needed for signing off each stage of the work.

However, it would is a mistake to presume that there is just one correct view of all systems development. Nowadays a more fluid approach is taken to the overall task which allows more freedom in allocating responsibility, work assignments and deliverables. A more general view is that the users must establish their purpose, express their needs, and then commission the development of the system, whether by procurement of a package or by bespoke systems development services. Clearly, with the portfolio model in mind, we will wish to adopt quite different approaches in each of its four segments. First, however, we must understand the traditional approach that is typical of systems development standards in organizations.

Project initiation

A project should not be started until there has been sufficient discussion about its purpose, timescales, the approach to be adopted and the authority required to see it through from start to finish.

Out of the initiation stage should come a simple feasibility report which states clearly the expected benefits, the cost and scheduling limitations, and how the project is to be resourced. There may be connections with, and dependencies upon, other projects working in related areas, and the balance of user and technical involvement needs to be planned. The scope of the project (in terms of the parts of the enterprise which are affected and the people who need to be involved) is fundamentally important to its success. The early planning will decide any need to go outside for ready-written software packages or for contract workers to provide special skills.

Needs analysis

Requirements analysis concerns the identification of user needs, problems and the expected benefits of the related application, in more detail than has previously been done. The main deliverables are a statement of the functional requirement (sometimes referred to as the user specification or the requirements specification), and at least the outline of an acceptance test plan which will stand as the main reference point during the later stage of acceptance testing.

Historically, this part of the overall process has been ill defined and fraught with difficulty and misunderstanding. Nowadays there are 'structured' methods for systems analysis which provide a degree of discipline and enable the process to be better understood. Needs analysis is very important to the success of the project and must be supported by appropriate time and effort. Any short cuts taken at this stage might save a little time or money in the short term but will incur orders of magnitude more cost before the project is successfully completed.

Because of their importance, the methods and techniques used for requirements analysis are discussed in more detail later in this chapter.

Technical design

Systems design concerns matching the requirement to different technical solutions. Typically it leads into programming, but at this stage it is necessary to consider any ready-written packages that are planned to be used, to look at interfaces with other existing systems, and possibly to consider the reuse of existing system components.

As well as producing a detailed technical specification for programming work (or the technical content of an invitation to tender in the case of package procurement), this activity should produce a system test plan which will stand as the main reference point during systems testing. It is possible at this stage to finalize the documentation which will support the system in use - both by the users themselves (the user manual), and in the case of larger systems the operations staff who run the computer room (the operations manual).

The design stage creates the bridge between the user's need and the hardware and software capability. It is concerned with mapping the business need (as recorded by the analysis work) into a technical solution, and with the addition of the physical design details which ensure that the system is reliable, secure and of adequate capacity.

System build (programming)

Out of this stage come program modules which (having first been tested individually) have to be brought together and tested together as a part of integration testing.

In the traditional model, this stage comprised the writing and testing of program code in a *programming language* such as 'COBOL', 'PL/I' or 'BASIC' - sometimes known as the 'third generation' languages or '3GLs'. These languages provide a syntax and a vocabulary which is used to make the computer do its job. They are still widely used for mundane systems development but newer languages for systems development (often referred to as 'fourth generation languages' or '4GLs') are less concerned with low-level coding. They allow higher level language statements which are much more powerful and more akin to natural language. Other new approaches to system building include the use of artificial intelligence tools ('fifth generation languages' - '5GLs') and object-oriented techniques. A brief overview is:

- *First and second generation languages* were widely used in the 1950s and 1960s and made little concession to the programmer, who had to be an expert. They use codes and highly constrained syntax which make them very difficult to understand. Today these very low-level languages are only used for writing operating systems software, and for other technical software components such as peripheral drivers and communications modules.

- *Third generation languages* made it easier to write computer programs by introducing 'ordinary' words with which to write programs, which now included such commands as

  ```
  COMPUTE NEW_BALANCE = OLD_BALANCE + TRANSACTION_AMOUNT
  ```

  which are easier to understand, but which are still limited in what they can do - the example would have to be applied to every posting to a ledger, for example. Nevertheless this reduced the cost of maintaining programs, and made it easier for programmers to share their work.

- *Fourth generation languages* provide - in a single command - the ability to do complete system tasks such as producing a printed report, updating a complete file, or merging different files together. For example:

```
REPLACE ALL BALANCE WITH BALANCE+AMOUNT FOR CREDIT='GOOD'
```

would apply all current transaction amounts to the whole accounts master file. This single command might have required ten to fifty 3GL commands, or even more.

- *Fifth generation languages* are based on the identification of the rules by which a business operates. They provide the means to embody these rules in a 'system' and reduce the time to construct a business application which depends of very complex logic (such as medical diagnosis) or involves vast quantities of data (such as military intelligence and battlefield data). A recent commercial example was concerned with the detection of credit card frauds, by detecting variations in the patterns of use.

- *The object orientation* is interesting because it reduces computer programs to the minimum of logic and data which is needed to deal with one thing, or 'object'. Thus a transaction record is seen as an abstract object which is subject to rules of product availability and customer credit, and which needs data about price and quantities. A customer record would be seen as all the rules needed to deal with customers throughout our involvement with them, and all the data about them. This rather abstract idea actually brings systems design much closer to reality, provided that we can help users to articulate ideas about objects which are meaningful at the business level. This technique is still at an early stage in its application to business systems design but is well established at the technical level. It leads to higher productivity and more maintainable systems, when it is properly used.

As can be seen from the brief description of how programming has evolved, the time taken in this stage of development is now diminishing. Most of the intellectually demanding work will have been done during analysis and design and the work of the programmer becomes less demanding as systems development techniques advance.

Integration testing

Software integration testing concerns the technical correctness and cohesion of the system. For example, it is necessary to ensure that the system complies with the technical specification, that it performs correctly and with adequate speed, and that it will not fail under the anticipated operating conditions because of workload or other considerations.

The integration test should be the subject of a plan which ensures that the basic 'function, fit and form' of the systems modules are as intended. Do all the modules work properly with each other? Can we be sure that the system will not print out a bill for £0.00p? What happens when the disk storage space runs out? What happens if the computer operator mounts the wrong magnetic tape file? These questions are all at the level of *how* the system works, rather than whether it does *what* the business needs.

Acceptance testing and system handover

The final stage is to satisfy the users that the system is ready for their use, and that it reflects all of the requirements that were originally specified. The system can then be handed over.

Acceptance testing is perhaps the least understood stage of development and there are no prescriptions as to how it shall be done. It may be a long time since the original requirement was specified and the business might have moved on. There may have been many changes of detailed requirements during the project, which will work against cohesion and completeness in the finished product.

Acceptance testing must be largely based upon the user's opinions to ensure that all is well. For example, is the system easy for them to use? Will all the expected benefits be achieved, given the delivered functionality and capability in the new system? Is the look and feel of the system right, and are the screen layouts and transaction dialogues appropriate for those who will have to work with the new system?

Realizing the benefits

This overview of the main stages started by stressing how important are the early stages of initiation and requirements analysis. Up to one third of the effort might typically be invested in these early stages in a successful project. It is surprising therefore that so little effort is put into assuring the realization of the benefits.

At the end of a typical project the users are happy to get the project team off their backs so that they can just get on with the job. It is enough simply to have to deal with the new system without analysing what benefits are coming from its use. Further, there are two stages to the full integration of any application into a business. First, users have to learn the simple skills involved in using the system: new equipment, new keyboards, new detailed business procedures and the like. Second (perhaps some months after handover), there will be an opportunity to adapt the way of working so as to gain secondary benefits.

For example, consider a new telephone sales order processing system. It might include facilities to automatically dial customer telephone numbers and to present much more information about customer's sales history, in order to speed up the process and to provide a more fully informed service to customers.

- In the first stage, the sales clerks will learn how to use the automatic dial facility and how to call for and understand the additional customer information. They are doing what they have always done, but more efficiently and more effectively.

- Later on, they will realize that the automatic dial 'directory' is a more effective way of dealing with all phone numbers and they will start to prefer it to the old paper directories. They may even lobby for the automatic dial facility to be extended to other parts of their work, for example in dealing with suppliers. Management will realize that the automatic dialling is a potential source of new management information about the nature and number of calls made, and to whom. Even more significant, customers will learn that the additional information about their sales history is readily available to their supplier, and start to change their approach to buying. They come to rely on it, and start to make ad hoc enquiries because the supplier has better information about their purchase history than they do.

In successfully managing the realization of benefits from information systems applications, it is important that this lifecycle of achievement is understood, that specific responsibility for managing the benefits is placed with an appropriate person, and that the secondary benefits are actively sought ought and maximised.

Responsibilities

This principle of placing responsibility applies to all the tasks in systems development. The V model gives us a view of the work to be done at four different levels, and this is likely to be reflected in the way in which we allocate responsibility for the work.

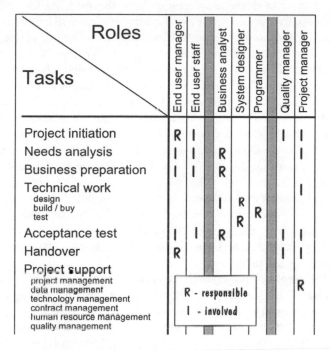

Tasks / Roles	End user manager	End user staff	Business analyst	System designer	Programmer	Quality manager	Project manager
Project initiation	R	I				I	I
Needs analysis	I	I	R				I
Business preparation	I	I	R				
Technical work							I
design			I	R			
build / buy					R		
test				R			
Acceptance test	I	I	R			I	I
Handover	R					I	I
Project support							R

R - responsible
I - involved

Project support
project management
data management
technology management
contract management
human resource management
quality management

Figure 7.3   Allocating roles and responsibilities

Figure 7.3 shows how the tasks of development might be assigned to the people involved. The detail may vary (we shall return to this later), but the shift in responsibility shown is important, illustrating how the user is involved at the start and the end, and the different technical skills in between.

Requirements analysis - one key to success

In the early days of systems development, requirements analysis was a 'black art'. It was so poorly understood that it was barely visible in the average project plan - programmers were simply set to work on programming without any attempt to understand the real needs first. However, nowadays it receives more attention than any other stage in systems development, and the methods and techniques employed are very refined. Graphical techniques are used to represent models of how the system will work. We might not be able to draw a picture of a new information system in the same way that we can draw a car or a house, but we can draw diagrams of how the information will move from one task to another and how the information will be structured.

Previously, the only graphic techniques for modelling systems were based on flowcharting symbols designed for the technician and signifying disk files, magnetic tape files and obsolete elements such as paper tape and punched card files. This is equivalent to presenting the house buyer with a detailed view of a house, one room at a time, with so much technical annotation about building materials and instructions that it is impossible for the inexpert eye to make a judgement about what is proposed. Happily, today we have a rich array of diagrammatic techniques to help. The general approach is to present a business level view of proposed systems which can be readily understood and debated, built to rules which are rigorous and which improve the quality of the work. The models that are used provide sufficient discipline to optimize the problem and avoid obvious traps at the same time that they make the specification process more visible to the users.

Consider one of the traps. A strong temptation is to use the organizational or geographic model to shape our thoughts about systems, such as the 'warehouse system', the 'personnel system', the 'head office system', or the 'Newcastle system'. However, it is no longer sensible to bound a system using organizational or geographic limits. The systems which provide an enterprise with real commercial advantage are those which are shared across the organization thereby permitting it to operate in a more integrated and timely way. The organizational model of an enterprise is not adequate as a foundation for the conception and definition of information systems and it actually leads to severe difficulties where function and data are to be shared.

A more considered approach to business modelling deals separately with:

- The organizational elements (departments, units, etc).
- The jobs that the people do (business function).
- The information that people work with (files and reports).
- The things of concern about which information is kept (customers, products, employees, branches).

Diagrammatic models can give an accurate representation of these different perspectives on the business. Just as we need to be able to see a new house from different perspectives if we are going to learn all about the internal, external and constructional arrangements, we need to see systems from several different points of view.

The key to good information systems requirements analysis is the ability to put aside the more traditional business models and to focus on *information*. Familiar diagramming techniques have been adapted to deal with this need and they have been incorporated into defined methods for development, redressing some of the imbalance towards technical issues. Further, there are now highly developed tools which support these methods and techniques making them more productive and manageable.

Methods, techniques and tools

A method for requirements analysis uses a defined set of activities and techniques which will, by and large, lead to information systems solutions in an orderly, manageable and repeatable manner. Most methods entirely embrace the requirements analysis phase; some also embrace the adjacent phases (feasibility before analysis, and design following).

At the time of writing, methods are offered mostly on a proprietary basis packaged with consultancy, technical support and training, but the detail of the different proprietary methods is converging and it is now increasingly within the public domain. The United Kingdom government has brought one particular method - Structured Systems Analysis and Design Method (SSADM) - into the public domain by requiring its use on all non-trivial central government projects. It is also used widely elsewhere.

As confidence in methods increases, and as more people gain the required skills, it must be expected that their use will become familiar to many business people. The tools supporting the new techniques for systems development are evolving quickly and provide 'repositories' for data about information systems. This means that it will be easier to catalogue, store and redeploy ideas about business systems without having to go through the full development cycle. Ideas about systems can be communicated more easily and more of the low-level systems development work will be automated. In due course they will permit a much more rapid development of the business information systems that are needed, with more of the development being undertaken by the users. However, we must not rush ahead. Instead we must make sure that we understand the principles which underpin the primary techniques and examples of the models which they produce.

The techniques fall into two categories, namely process analysis techniques and information analysis techniques. Both kinds of technique can be learned easily by business people as well as by technical specialists. Proprietary systems are based upon these two approaches and may show a bias towards one or the other. For example, proprietary methods from the USA are predominantly process driven; in Europe there has been a much stronger interest in information analysis, especially in the United Kingdom, France and the Netherlands.

Terminology

Terminology in this area is not universally agreed and there are conflicting uses of terms such as 'process', 'function', 'information' and 'data'. In particular the advent of such strong interest in business process management (and redesign, and re-engineering) has put a new focus on the word 'process'. There is no universal definition even within the BPR literature.

Here, we shall use certain key words as follows:

- *'Entity'* refers to any element of a business about which we wish to keep information (for example: customers, suppliers, products, employees, sales, problems, and so on).

- *'Information'* refers to the aggregation of data that - when it is interpreted and understood - provides systems users with knowledge of some kind (for example: invoice, pay slip, stock exception report, and so on).

- *'Process'* refers to that collection of activities or steps which takes information as input, manipulates it in some way, and presents the results as output (for example: the sales order process, new product design, employee appraisal, and so on). Note that many people use the words *process, activity, task* and *step* in quite specific ways; here we simply use the word *process* unless there is good reason not to do so .

Each of these definitions can be used at higher and lower levels. When determining information systems strategies it will be useful to lay down high-level entity models which help to delineate the boundaries of the business: a retailer might wish to explore what the consequences of extending the business systems to include customer information, as in the introduction of 'loyalty cards'. When analysing the detail of one critical business process, it will be broken down into lower level processes until we have the level of precision that will properly deal with discounting rules, or quality control procedures.

Why don't you tell me what goes on here, then?

OK, if you really want to know! I have a number of people reporting to me dealing with selling, cold calling, re-ordering and sales reporting. They change so quickly, though. As soon as we have someone up to speed they rush off and work for someone else. It follows that we spend a great deal of time recruiting new staff - it's a terrible problem round here and we have to go the full round of advertising, interviewing and so on. I've got salesmen on the road (and women - Janet is in day-to-day charge of the sales force), I've got sales assistants in the showroom and one trusty clerk who keeps me on the straight and narrow. She's called Susan and she's excellent! I couldn't manage without her - she takes charge of the adverts for new hires, and writes all the rejection letters for me. She also arranges the interviewing schedules and deals with the personnel department when I want to offer a job.

Sometimes when there is a crisis I get involved with the travelling and I let one of the sales folk come in and interview the salesroom candidates; nevertheless it's still my responsibility to oversee the interviews and to have the final say in offering jobs. I suppose I also get involved in the wording of the adverts for new staff because the details frequently change, but really I leave most of all that to Susan.

But that's just the staff management side. The selling is what it's really all about. We've got people on the road as I said, who are chasing up new business and dealing direct with the big clients. The staff in the salesroom do the over the-counter business which makes up the majority of our revenue. I insist on approving all the sales trips and I sometimes insist on going along - for example when the salesman is new or when the client situation is critically important. Then when a big deal is struck I generally go along to join in the merriment! I have to sign off all deals over a certain level, and all those closed by the junior sales people. That's the part I enjoy most. The paperwork is a real drag though. Can't stand it myself. Leave all of that to Susan - she chases up the monthly sales reports from the sales folk and does the area and regional analyses which lead to a summary report for me and my boss. I'm supposed to check it before it goes off but I don't bother. Susan does it all beautifully. What I do have to do is chase up the damned sales people. They never do what they're told, even for Susan.

I was talking about the sales effort, wasn't I? Yes well, when a salesman is organizing a trip they have to make up there own minds how to go about it and I just check it over (mostly so that I can keep a check on the expense accounts). Susan helps with the travel arrangements when bookings have to be made and she is very involved with the deals. When we are getting near to closing she prepares the draft contracts for us. Sometimes we even have to prepare tenders. Anyway, it falls to Susan to do the paperwork and luckily she's a real whiz with the word processor. She whips out the last one we did and changes the odd word here and there. Terrific stuff, this technology, eh? ....

I guess so ... !

Process example: narrative form

Process analysis

The overall function of a business application can be very complex, but the process viewpoint is a very natural one for people working in the business and the analysis of business processes often provides the most fruitful starting point. Users tend to be action oriented and warm more quickly to a discussion about *what they do* rather than the abstract structure of the information they are dealing with. There are two kinds of diagram frequently associated with function analysis, namely the *process decomposition diagram* and the *flow diagram* (often referred to as a data flow diagram). The first shows how high-level processes are made up from lower level processes, and the second shows how information flows between them.

Here we will illustrate their use based upon the rather chaotic operations within a local builders merchant business, looking at showroom and external sales operations (see narrative example in the box 'A process example').

Decomposition diagrams

The generic decomposition diagram deals with problems of complexity by dividing the problem into parts, one level at a time. A familiar example is the organization chart which shows how a company is divided into divisions, which are subdivided into departments, which are then further divided into groups, and so on down to individuals. Another less familiar example is a bill of materials, which shows how a complex product is divided into assemblies, subassemblies and components.

In information systems requirements analysis, decomposition diagrams are used frequently to show the structure of the processes within a system, both at the higher levels (overall business process) and at the lower levels (structure of individual clerical processes and computer programs).

Figure 7.4 provides a simple example based on the builders merchant. From the details we can see that the showroom recruits its own staff, has responsibility for some stock management and is involved in over the counter sales as well as account development. It also produces some management information. The decomposition diagram is a powerful device useful in the earliest stages of specifying a system to tabulate in a structured way all that goes on; it can be seen how much more quickly it can be understood that the narrative example.

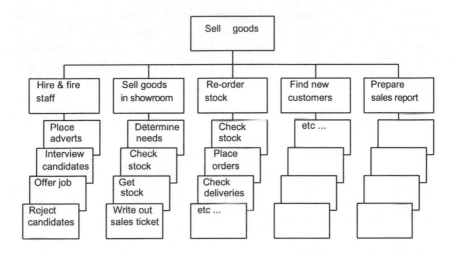

Figure 7.4 Process modelling example: decomposition diagram

It provides the basis for the initial scoping of a project at a detailed level. The example provides a framework for cataloguing operational business problems and opportunities; it provides the basis of a discussion about how extensive the system should be, and helps us to anticipate who needs to be involved in the needs analysis.

Each of the main 'branches' of this decomposition can be analysed for the flow of data into and out of its low-level processes.

Data flow diagram

Data flow diagrams show how data (and sometimes goods) flow from one point in a business (a point of storage or distribution, say) to another (such as sales). The rules for developing data flow diagrams are relatively simple and everyone should be able to understand them if they are constructed properly and presented carefully. Users can check the diagrams for completeness and accuracy far more easily than the pages and pages of textual description which are the only real alternative. Users will often choose to get involved with the development of the diagrams whether informally by reaching for the pen during interviews with the analyst, or by assuming complete responsibility for them - although this cannot be done without proper training.

Consider the further detail of the example. Figure 7.5 provides additional details about just one of the legs in the tree structure - that dealing with the showroom operations (the other branches of the business process model will each have their own flow diagram). It shows the flow of goods (using bold lines) as well as information (using thinner lines), and places where the goods and information are stored.

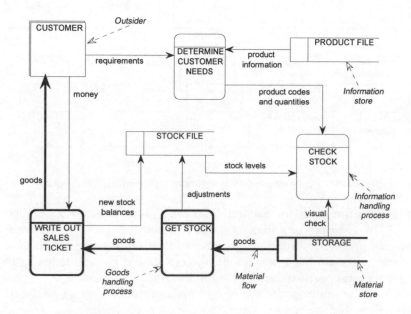

Figure 7.5   Process modelling example: data flow diagram

The four components of data flow diagrams (see the annotations in Figure 7.5) are:

- processes (which achieve the transformation of inputs to outputs, dealing with information and goods, or just information)
- flows (information and goods on the move)
- stores (information and goods at rest)
- outsiders (people and organizations outside the system boundary)

Data flow diagrams are developed using rules which govern how they are drawn, how they relate to one another, and how they relate to the more detailed specification material which supports them. While management will not be involved routinely in creating them, it behoves everyone in a business to learn how to read them and how to make judgements about their quality, cohesion and completeness.

The diagrams given here are merely illustrative of the way function decomposition and data flow diagrams are used. In a real case a function decomposition would be more likely to show between fifty lower level processes (in a small system) through to several hundred (in a large system). There might be twenty data flow diagrams in a medium-sized system showing details of about one hundred and fifty processing elements, and the information which flow within and among them. The total number of detailed system components (processes, flows, stores and outsiders) in these twenty data flow diagrams could be as many as one thousand.

Information analysis

The other kind of analysis is concerned with information, and almost completely ignores the functionality of the system. Information analysis is a demanding discipline which is founded in mathematical theory (the 'relational algebra') and it is beyond the scope of this book to deal with it in any detail. At the lower level of detail it is often referred to as 'data analysis'.

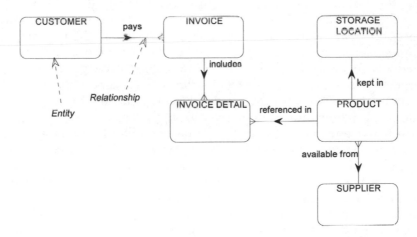

Figure 7.6 Information modelling example: entity model

Figure 7.6 provides a very simple example of its essential result: the *entity model*. These diagrams can be developed in two ways:

- From the bottom up, by the analysis of operational business information as it appears in routine documents and reports, based upon minute inspection of those documents and protracted negotiation about the meaning and significance of the data contained therein. This is a tortuous process that can consume many man years of effort. If the purpose is to find new business ideas, it is not a productive approach.

- From the top down, by asking senior management to identify the key elements of the business about which they want to keep information. This can be very rapid, and it is best done by brainstorming. In just a few minutes a meeting can get a firm grip on the most unusual ideas, given good facilitation. Obviously it is most useful when we are looking for new ideas rather than for simple operational improvements.

The entity model tells us nothing about the dynamic behaviour of a business but a lot about the underlying relationships between its fundamental components. The essential definition of an entity is: '*any thing about which we may wish to keep information*'. In the entity model all these things are seen in the same way but they may represent quite different kinds of 'thing': people (customer, employee), organizations (operating company, regulatory body), product (stock item, non-stock item), locations (shelf, head office), moments in time (approval, sale), or even completely abstract notions (project, idea). This ability to render such disparate things equal in information terms is the main strength of the entity model, because it helps is to break the mould of conventional thinking. Instead of arguing the case for a new system for the financial controller, or for the Scandinavian warehouse, we can see the system for what it really is: a means of manipulating information in support of business processes which may transcend departmental and geographical boundaries.

An important property of these entity models is that they reduce our vision of the system idea to just one page of paper. Even for the most complex businesses it is possible to contain a complete view of the entities on a single page. Almost every other perspective requires many pages to accommodate all the detail, leading to all the consequent problems of understanding and checking of details.

Note how one can 'read' the entity model (see Figure 7.6), for example 'CUSTOMER pays INVOICE'. The relationships between entities hint at the processes that we will need in the business to service them: processes to deal with customer enquiries and to receive payments. The explicit details of these processes are to be found in the process decomposition and the flow models.

Variations on a theme

Although there has been a history of difficulty with the development of information systems, the basic processes which must be undertaken are now well understood and are being widely adopted. In recent years the following kinds of argument have become quite familiar:

- The development of complex systems needs the sort of discipline that is inherent in the world of engineering.

- A system needs to be thought of as an assembly of parts, each of which is properly constructed to fit in with the others, rather than as a homogeneous whole.

- The process of systems development is more manageable when it follows the traditional engineering project cycle of requirements analysis, technical design, construction and testing.

Systems development that does not incorporate these kinds of ideas is impossible to estimate accurately and can result in systems of poor quality, which perform inefficiently and which are difficult to maintain. However, this is not enough. Today systems are needed far more quickly in order to react to rapidly changing circumstances or to seize competitive advantage. Users are more aware of systems principles and want to take more responsibility for doing their own thing. At the same time the complexity of some systems is greater than ever and we task the ability of the most capable systems people to deal with them.

Dealing with systems development problems

Systems development has been seen for at least twenty years in a rather singular way. For many years the differences between different kinds of project seemed to be of no great concern and one can quote examples where projects which were experimental in nature were given the full treatment - armies of technical designers and programmers working to very rigorous standards - and on the other hand there were critically important projects that were implemented on a 'wing and a prayer'.

In the face of any difficulty, the inclination in the past has been to introduce more particular standards, more rules and more procedures, in order to tighten up the way that systems were being produced. This is appropriate in some cases but not in all. The analysis of current and future potential of systems using the strategic grid (see Figure 6.1) gives a portfolio model which is very enlightening and extremely effective in planning the detail of development projects. The paragraphs below review it again and interpret systems development in each quadrant, expanding upon some of the introductory comments made in the early part of Chapter 6. Some current ideas for systems development such as prototyping, outsourcing and package acquisition can then be mapped back into the portfolio model and explained in relation to the V model.

High potential

A small proportion of high potential applications will ultimately provide strategic opportunities and help to secure the future of the company. An organization which refuses to accept the need for high potential activity will have great difficulty making progress in the face of competitive and economic forces, whereas one which nurtures and sustains experimentation will never be short of sound, well qualified and potentially useful systems ideas.

How does one go about systems development in this quadrant? Not with meticulous attention to standards, nor even with large teams of technicians drafted in to make up the numbers. Development in this part of the strategic grid has to be done by (or in very close conjunction with) the user whose idea it is. The objective is not to change the world, but to qualify an idea as a good one. Once this qualification is achieved, when everyone agrees that the idea is important and when the rest of the company has agreed to take it on board, then the style of development will have to change. However, until it is qualified development needs to be fluid, exploratory, and as rapid as possible. There is no benefit in protracted development; every effort should be directed towards the qualification of the idea and as quickly as possible. If the idea proves to be a good one then it can be progressed, but if it is not then it can be discarded. Survival in high potential systems development activity is just as much about learning to live with failure as well as enjoying success.

Strategic

The strategic systems development project needs to have the total support and commitment of the user management and staff. The development of the requirements analysis must be done with the business in mind, and with more attention to what might be done in the future than what is done now. Thus *business* analysts are required, not technical analysts. A good business analyst is difficult to find and even the best technician - given responsibility for the conception and specification of a strategic system - will create difficulties all round. Business analysis might be difficult in the strategic context and rather than expecting users to straightforwardly explain their needs, a degree of iterative prototyping might replace conventional analysis, as shown in Figure 7.7.

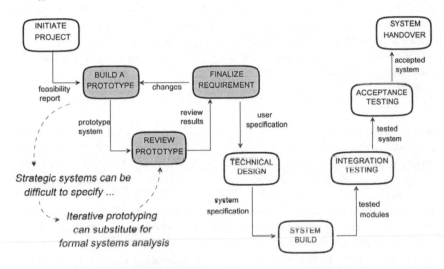

Figure 7.7 Adapting the V model to strategic projects

A technical systems analyst must be trained in business skills in order to make a useful contribution in the development of strategic systems. Further, the tools that are used by the analyst must be appropriate. It will be necessary to formulate and model ideas about the new system from fairly flimsy ideas seeded in corporate objectives, critical success factors, and the other stuff of strategic analysis. It is important, therefore, that the analysts are able to create good business models which will help all those involved to assure themselves that the proposals are complete and appropriate.

The construction stage in the strategic development project cannot afford to get bogged down in detailed work, but equally it cannot be cut short. The system must work and to some extent it will have to integrate with existing systems, but not at a very detailed and complex level. It is important that strategic systems are built quickly and competently. Efficiency in their operation is not as important as effectiveness, but nevertheless, the development team must try to forecast the workload levels and ensure that there is enough computer power to sustain the system, even if later it will be re-engineered to make it more efficient.

Testing of the system is important also. There must be carefully prepared test plans which will allow the user to test the function and facility of the system, and to demonstrate its quality and capability against the original requirements specification. Finally, at handover, it will probably be quite impractical to undertake 'parallel running' because of the changes which the system brings. One day the old system is used and the next day the new one is used. Trying to live with two systems running concurrently is meaningless when they do not necessarily function in the same way.

Key operational

There are fewer mysteries to the key operational system. The application is likely to be well known, it is probably common to all the main players in a certain industry, and there may well be packages available which provide a suitable vehicle for implementation (although they are not always cheap - six-figure US$ prices are common for the larger mainframe packages). The larger, more forward thinking companies often find themselves putting these systems together first, the hard way. In fact they may be seen the first time around as strategic because only the larger companies can afford the very high development costs and they justify the expense on the basis of consolidating their dominance of the market. When the ideas have matured the systems then become available from software suppliers (sometimes in the form of a modification of the original system developed by a main player), or if preferred they can be developed in-house more cheaply because the application has become better known and there will be people around who can be hired for their experience and knowledge of the application.

Thus, development projects which are dealing with key operational applications systems may find packages to be more suitable than bespoke development. The system still needs to be specified, however, because a good package will provide many options and there will be work to do in setting it up properly. Although a package is the primary vehicle for implementation, it still has to be evolved into the end-users' application system. It is a mistake to confuse the two. If a user decides that problems will be solved by putting in someone else's application system, then they will almost certainly fail. Even the best package will lead to some programming work because other key operational applications systems will have to co-exist with the new one and will need to be adapted to interface with it. As some of us already know, adapting an existing system can be much more difficult than building a new one from scratch. On the other hand, the best packages can be seen as indicative of good business practice and we find that large companies (for example Tesco and ASDA Superstores in the UK) choose to use the same package (in this case, a US-originated package called World Wide Chain Stores) for their core stock management and purchase order processing. This does not mean that the businesses have to be the same: the package just deals with the core information processing requirements at the operational level. This leaves plenty of scope for differentiation at the strategic level, with other more adventurous applications.

The analysis of a key operational system can be done by specialists rather than by generalists, i.e. the technical specialist is probably more appropriate here than the business analyst. The technical skills become very important because efficiency and resilience in a key operational system are important. Depending upon the hardware and software environment, skilled database and teleprocessing specialists will be needed, and also systems programmers who can tune the mainframe to give the last percentage point in efficiency. At the testing and handover stage, parallel running will probably be a better approach because we are trying to maintain rather than change the status quo and we need to be sure that the new system produces the same essential outputs.

Support systems

Support systems are in some senses the most difficult to generalize. They are systems which have little or no current or future strategic relevance, and the temptation is to invest a minimum and to go wherever possible for absolutely standard packages even if they do not fit well - the presumption being that we can change the way we do things to fit the package. Using a package obviates the need to do detailed design and program development, and the effect on the standard V model is shown in Figure 7.8.

Consider an application dealing with Statutory Sick Pay (SSP) record keeping requirements in the United Kingdom, for example. This is a legal requirement on employers to keep certain data about their employees' sickness leave. It is unlikely that anyone, other than a software house selling personnel management packages, is going to see this as strategically important - the personnel department of a typical company can almost certainly be persuaded to fit its procedures around a standard SSP package, although the personnel staff may really believe that they ought to have a special system of their own. There are some cautionary points to be noted, however.

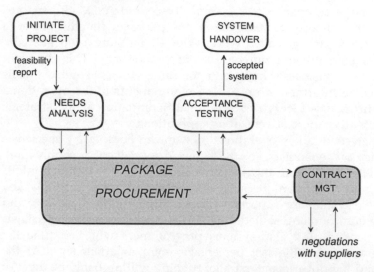

Figure 7.8 Adapting the V model to support projects

For example, a support system needs a degree of requirements analysis to be certain that it is truly a support system. Interfaces with other systems must be investigated because any strong links to key operational or strategic systems might affect our view of things - perhaps the support system is not a support system at all? The users' commitment must be assessed to ensure that they really require the system and that they are willing to manage the development project and deal with procurement of packages and the ultimate cut-over to the new system. Support systems do not justify the use of scarce, skilled systems development resources which are deployed more usefully in the other three strategic quadrants.

Having said this, we might remember classic examples such as the American Hospital Supplies case, which started with a single customer who wanted to go online because his sales rep noticed they used the same kind of terminal. A support project, surely, as it was originally conceived, but so obviously strategic when later seen in the competitive context! We must always remember that the classification of applications can change over time, either because of a change in the business context, or because we simply choose to regard it differently when it makes business sense to do so.

Horses for courses

What we have learned from the above review of the strategic grid is that there cannot be and must not be a singular view of the systems development task. It is essential that there is some flexibility so that the profile of each development project can be specified individually with appropriate tools and technical skills, and the right degree of user involvement. Indeed, at one end of the scale we must provide for users who want to do their own thing, and at the other we must provide for meticulously built core systems which will be efficient, reliable and economic to maintain.

Regrettably there is little evidence that the typical information systems department sees it this way, although there are examples of companies which provide facilities for end-user computing and 'multiple choice' paths for large scale systems development. This provides some basis upon which to incorporate the ideas of the strategic grid.

The effect of providing choice is to promote the importance of project management. Whether it is the end user or a large team of people, the risk that it goes wrong can outweigh the benefits of providing flexibility. It is essential to classify and plan projects within the overall applications portfolio in a way that is appropriate to the business needs and the available resources. It is possible to channel and take advantage of the user's enthusiasm and to optimize the deployment of scarce central technical resources. However, by providing options the risk that we choose the wrong approach is increased.

From the basic V model for systems development (see Figure 7.2) we could either develop a much more detailed approach to development - the rigorous engineering approach - or we could relax it somewhat. We might replace one of the seven basic stages with an alternative procedure which gives flexibility where needed. We might wish to acquire a package or we might just wish to work to a simpler model.

Prototyping

Prototyping is becoming more useful to the world of business information systems as the methods and tools that make it possible become better understood. In order to understand what is involved consider a prototype motor car, which is built as an approximation to the intended final product but not in the same way as a production car. It incorporates enough of the design ideas for the final product so that the design can be validated and the car rendered manufacturable. Essentially, a prototype is functional and it works, but it is not intended for sale and use by regular customers.

The same argument can be adopted in developing information systems. A prototype can be developed which is 'quick and dirty' and which helps to clarify the detail of the requirement when it is uncertain what is required at a detailed level (for example in strategic applications). Having developed the prototype, it will probably be thrown away and the proper system built in the conventional way (see Figure 7.7). However, we may choose to keep the prototype and use it, even though this is high risk, but this may suit our needs when we are exploring the potential benefits of high potential systems. Prototyping is an approach that will suit end-user computing where the development task is localized, informal and low risk.

In choosing to prototype we are discarding the basis for control over the phases of our project - and reducing the clarity with which we can measure and assess progress. We have to be certain, therefore, that the scope of the project is clear and that there are some alternative controls in place. The primary mechanism for control would normally be the review process where the prototype is assessed for features and capabilities, and compared with the results of a previous review - so long as we can see change we can argue that progress is being made. Alternatively, we can take the cruder approach of applying cash or time limits to force a conclusion to a prototyping project.

The engineering approach

The opposite to prototyping is to put in much more detail in the project plan, apply more control, and invest more heavily in project management. This might be termed the engineering approach because it uses the same meticulous approach which engineers adopt in the large complex projects in other areas, such as large construction and electrical engineering projects. The effect on the V model diagram is to add a great deal of detail.

This is not appropriate for medium and small sized companies where the costs cannot be tolerated because it is easy to double or treble the cost of a project undertaken in this way. It might suit the purposes of a software house, a bank or an airline, however. In the software house, the engineering approach is the only way in which a high level of quality and maintainability can be assured and the costs in this case can be offset against lower support and maintenance costs in the longer term. Should it fail, an airline system might affect the safety of people and a banking system might jeopardize the security of money which is invested. Therefore, for these sorts of reason the expensive engineering approach will be justifiable. It is likely that in future safety critical systems will have to be developed to very exacting standards.

Buying a package

Another more common situation is the purchase of a package - either ready to run or as a bespoke system (see Figure 7.8). When someone else does the detailed design and programming work we can avoid getting involved in this expensive activity, and a package will be fully tested on handover if it is from a reputable source. By eliminating the detail of design and programming the effect on the basic V model diagram is visually the same as prototyping, but in substance it is very different. A degree of requirements analysis will still be needed although too much analysis will work against our interests, because there is less likelihood that a suitable package will be found. It is better that a well known package is chosen which is based upon good business practice, to which the business can be adapted. Very often a business can be improved in this way. Computerizing a business mess will merely produce a computerized mess - better to buy a package that helps to tidy up.

Third parties are introduced as soon as a package is considered, so there are other jobs to be done. Contracts must be drafted and approved, quality controls put in place and (when buying a bespoke system) progress reporting procedures implemented which will ensure all parties communicate effectively.

Outsourcing

Another option is to use outside staff or services for some or all of a project. This might be because there is a high level of demand during a transition of some kind or because it is standard policy. We would not wish to outsource critical strategic work but it makes a good deal of sense to outsource non-critical maintenance and support work.

There are software and systems service providers who specialize in outsourcing and applied intelligently it will undoubtedly help the business. Regrettably and largely because of a failure to understand the principles of the applications portfolio outsourcing has been used in the wrong situation. It has also been used without specifying the extent of the responsibilities being outsourced. With the portfolio model and a proper work breakdown structure based on the V model and the other business tasks to be done it is possible to avoid these difficulties and to use outsourcing successfully.

End-user computing

Like outsourcing, end-user computing is a special consideration which can undermine the effectiveness of information systems if not properly managed. There are two kinds of end-user computing - first, entirely local systems which are implemented with spreadsheet and other general purpose software tools, and second decision support systems which rely on access to data from operational systems.

In the first case it helps to provide standard packages with which the users can work. This ensures that a proper level of help and support can be provided and it can economize the cost by volume purchase agreements. In the second case there are wider issues of access control, data integrity and ownership, information centre organization and management, and the need to provide basic definitions of the meaning of different data types.

The role of the information centre dedicated to the support of end users is a developing one. The idea that we can economize by providing specialist support is an attractive one. If users can be supported in an appropriate degree of self help activity the specialists can be deployed more effectively - ratios of 1:70 or more are quoted. By organizing end-user computing with limited central support up to seventy users can be supported adequately by each specialist. Naturally, the skills of these specialists have to be considered - the average programmer will not do. Someone with patience and an ability to talk to the end user in the users' language is needed. At the same time they must have an instinct for the end-user application which is actually the tip of some corporate iceberg (it is essential that substantive systems development is not hidden in the guise of a local support system) and they must be able to solve technical problems originating in complex mixtures of hardware, systems software, applications software and networking equipment.

Summary

Deciding how to reconcile the approach to systems development with the applications portfolio is no trivial task, but the general nature of what can be done should now be more clear (see Table 7.1 below). Where users are involved, they must understand and commit to their involvement.

Table 7.1   Systems development and the applications portfolio

	High potential	Strategic	Key operational	Support
Project definition	Loose and open. Cost limits rather than firm objectives.	Strong, management led team. Broad brief including business changes. Use strategic tools for the job.	Technical leadership, tight definition of standards. Meticulous project management.	Use external services if possible. Let the user manage the project.
Analysis of requirement	Exploratory and informal. Use prototyping to establish details.	Creative and broad in scope. Carefully document the work. Lots of reviews.	Contained but thorough. Attention to interfaces. Aim for efficiency in the system.	Limit to essential needs and ensure the isolation of the system from others.
System build	Rapid and iterative. Use peer reviews to identify weaknesses and opportunities	Innovative but carefully planned and rapid. Limited prototyping.	Contract out, or use packages where possible. Aim for efficiency.	Avoid undue effort. Contract out and use packages.
System test	Informal.	Well planned with an eye to the business issues.	Exhaustive, with a bias to the technical and the efficiency of the system.	To a degree, assume that it works. Minimal central effort, leave as a local responsibility.
Handover	Crossed fingers? Users must rely on their own judgement.	With great care! The big-bang approach may be the only way. Lots of education.	With great care! Parallel run to ensure the accuracy of outputs and compatibility with other systems.	Minimize effort and ensure user self-sufficiency.

When everything comes together properly the results can be spectacular. The important message is that it is not appropriate to treat all development projects in the same way. The incorporation of prototyping ideas will help in the upper part of the strategic grid and packages are likely to be more helpful in the lower half of the grid. Where systems are critical, sound information systems engineering methods are needed; where systems are not critical, a more casual approach is in order.

8

Support for the system development process

Introduction

Traditionally most attention has been paid to systems development as distinct from systems operation; in fact, the full lifetime cost including the operational phase will be far greater than the initial development costs. A very high proportion of the total cost of a system can be attributed to the operational stage (typically 70%), and this cost accrues to the user.

Much of it is avoidable. We are still learning how to build information systems that are more robust and more easily maintained, and there is in any case less need to build our own bespoke systems. It is now possible to acquire large and very capable software packages for routine needs (payroll, accounting, stock management and the like). The advantages of buying a package include the fact that someone else will maintain it, at a known cost.

It follows that the 'information systems resource' is much more than what we see in the development stages. We might start with the completed systems which are operational. All of the output from the development process is resource (specifications, programs, manuals and even test plans). The tools of systems development and maintenance (programming language systems, analysis and design tools, library management systems and all the supporting systems software) are also part of the IS resource, in the same way that plant and equipment is the essential resource of a manufacturing company.

Many people argue today that we need to take an 'inventory' approach to managing the IS resource, and some (in the United States and elsewhere) even talk of devising a standard part-numbering scheme for systems and software products which would allow them to be shared by *all* interested parties (much as is now done in the retail food trade through the use of universal product codes).

People as a resource

There is another aspect of the IS resource, the people who are involved. Competent technical staff who have the skills to develop and maintain systems are still in short supply and are likely to continue to be so. In easing the problems of resourcing individual projects it is important to consider user staff (who want the system) as part of the resource and to involve them productively in the work that has to be done. This leads naturally on to the issue of how the various human resources are organized and to whom they report in the organization.

How much resource should be deployed centrally and how much away from the centre? This has been a major issue and a source of conflict for many years. It is partly a matter of control and accountability, partly about the most effective means of supply management and partly about ownership of the resources and the resulting systems. Effective ways of managing these aspects of information systems resource are considered in the second half of this chapter.

IT management issues

There are many management issues inherent in keeping the IS resource together and in making sure that we deploy our efforts in an optimum way. Consider some of the following:

- The information system is made up of very large numbers of technical components or elements (program code, communications equipment, personal computers, mainframe hardware and systems software) which can be thought of collectively as an asset which needs managing just like any other.

- The system performs business functions and supports business processes. These are always likely to change and the supporting systems need to be kept relevant to these changing needs.

172

- There is documentation which describes the systems and their components, and which stands as the reference point when we wish to do change or enhance them - documentation (especially for key operational systems) must always be updated meticulously and kept up to the same change level as the system it describes.

- The information systems workforce is in constant need of training and updating - we need to organize and deploy the scarce personnel resources that we do have optimally and set appropriate priorities to new development and maintenance work.

- The security of our systems is a key issue. Some of the components of information systems are extremely vulnerable to malevolence and to acts of God, especially the data when stored on exchangeable media. It is essential to be able to recover from disasters of all kinds.

- As systems become dispersed physically, the whole question of their cohesion and compatibility becomes a major problem: which components work with which others? Does something which works on one computer work on another (probably not)? How many versions of a program or systems specification have we got? As networking becomes more widespread the need to keep the network in good shape becomes a significant task.

- The capacity of installed computer equipment (such as large mainframes and networks) to do work is very complex to estimate and manage. Capacity management is a special skill which is not easily found.

- How do we manage changes and problems when (either in operation or in development) someone decides that the objectives have changed or that we have actually got it wrong and created a problem that needs solving?

- The maintenance of systems in use is, as already mentioned, a considerable task which typically costs more than half of the IS budget.

Security

Security is one of today's major issues as systems become more global, more dependent on networks, and therefore more accessible to those with mischievous intentions. Detection is difficult because machine-readable data can easily be copied. The complex nature of computer-based information systems helps to make the detection of criminal activity extremely difficult. It almost always comes to light by accident, and many organizations prefer not to deal with computer crime in the courts in case it undermines external confidence in their corporate and management skills. Worst of all, it is possible to perpetrate a computer crime without entering any corporate premises. Any computer that is connected to the public telephone network or even to privately owned but external transmission cables is at risk of unauthorized access.

The operation and management of systems which are in use is quite different from managing the development process. An information systems project is much like any other: a collection of different people with different skills, assigned temporarily to a shared task. An IT operations department is likely to be organized along functional lines which recognize and maintain the different IT skills. The gulf between the project staff (who just want to rush off to the next project) and the operational staff (who work on many tasks at the same time, on much shorter timescales) can be as great as the gulf between IT generally and the business.

The modern business depends so completely upon its information technology that short-term pressures can be over-riding. The management of operational information systems is done from one moment to the next as minor operational crises come and go. The longer-term operational concerns such as security and the need to be able to recover from major disasters are often pushed to the background thereby putting the whole organization needlessly at risk. This is another balancing act for management to struggle with.

Comparison with other resource management issues

Much of the IS resource management challenge can be seen as similar to that seen elsewhere. Consider manufacturing management. The same attitudes and skills that are successful in managing a stores area containing valuable components will probably help us to deal with the IS 'inventory' with equal success. But the nature of the product we are concerned with is unique and means that:

- because it is abstract there is no immediate common basis upon which different parties can easily share their views of what a system is;

- it is possible to change software very quickly indeed and to leave absolutely no evidence that the changes have been made;

- it is very complex, the most simple systems being based upon thousands of elemental components and large systems being based upon millions;

- the context within which we conceive and build systems can change rapidly.

The need for supporting disciplines

In order to get an understanding of the potential difficulties that arise from the nature of the product, and the differences when compared with ordinary material product, this chapter provides a review of six key activities or supporting disciplines that must be present if the development and use of information systems is to succeed.

Supporting disciplines for information systems

The systems development community have adopted and adapted a number of management disciplines originally developed elsewhere. They embrace the management of documentation and changes; project and quality management, capacity management and security.

Documentation management

Although software may exist in a material sense on a disk or some other storage medium, this is a machine-readable representation which is of no use to a person who wishes to know the nature, purpose or function of the software. Whereas in a moment we can identify the nature and purpose of a car (and distinguish it from a lorry or a bus), it is impossible to determine the purpose and nature of a system when looking at the disk that contains it.

It falls to the paperwork to tell us what a system does for us and how it does it. No doubt many people have suffered the frustration of having to learn how to use software which was not properly documented. If we are acquiring software today one of our primary concerns is the quality of the documentation which accompanies it and the way in which it will help with installation and use.

How often have we stopped to consider the other documentation that must support a software system? Consider for example the problems of people working in the software development team. They have to rely on documentation:

- to provide a single definition of the developing system;
- to ensure that different modules in the system work properly with each other when they are put together; and
- to demonstrate the extent of progress being made to project leaders and management.

The role of documentation in achieving all of this is critical. It is primarily through the documentation that a system is rendered comprehensible.

A system which is to have any significant lifetime of use has to be documented 'for the record' so that it can be improved and extended. Even the personal computer user who is developing a personal spreadsheet needs to have some record of what has been done, if the spreadsheet is of any significant size and if it is not a one-off. In the case of large complex systems it is critically important that the system is well documented if it is going to be developed further in the future. In all but the most trivial situations it is necessary to provide standards for documentation which will give basic helpful guidance to all those using a system. The content and scope of use of each kind of document needs to be clearly understood.

Above all it is the needs of the reader which must be kept in mind. It is not uncommon to find that an IS department has technical standards that deal only with development documentation. User documentation must be provided to help those concerned to use the system. Even better, put the documentation on the computer itself, and 'publish' it through the computer and the terminals which people use, so that a computer-based support system can help by the use of automatic indexes, by providing different levels of access and different levels of detail. Users are quickly coming to accept that the help systems provided with packaged software is all that they need to be able to use modern software - bespoke systems must provide the same level of support.

We can summarize the purpose of documentation as follows:

- To provide a human-readable representation of a system for those concerned with its development or maintenance.
- To record the final form of the system as loaded onto the machine.
- To communicate the state of development to other interested parties.
- To record the final form of the system as loaded onto the computer itself.

- To place on record the function and capability of a completed system for the benefit of those who might wish later to correct, improve or enhance it.

- To make available the information and instructions needed by the users of the system.

Software change management

As we come to rely more upon old systems which cannot easily be replaced and new systems which are complex and modular we find a need to manage software changes and different release versions. It is the difficulty in managing changing systems which undermines our ability to keep pace with the needs of business. Dealing with changes can be a most difficult task. Changes may be raised by the user (because the business has changed), or by the technical staff (because the technology or implementation strategy has changed, or because bugs in the system have been detected).

When there are many to be dealt with it is important that changes are not dealt with on an individual basis. They must be evaluated in the overall context of the system and its status (using the technical documentation that is to hand), grouped into remedial work packages and then handled as mini-projects in their own right. Without this process of rationalization the work that derives from uncontrolled changes can wreck the quality and cohesion of an otherwise excellent maintenance plan, and rapidly undermine the viability of an installed system in the operational phase. One fault can lead to many fault reports; if each fault report becomes a separate remedial action there will be chaos. Equally, a number of user change requests might all be related so that they can be dealt with by one single action. If they are dealt with separately, the coherency of the system will be undermined as similar features are provided in different places within it. This becomes a nightmare for anyone who has to maintain the system. It is rumoured that one large UK bank has eighteen different places where it keeps a customer's name and address, and a well known computer manufacturer had seventeen different ways to raise a purchase order. In each case it is probably the result of inadequate change and version control.

Security management

Security and privacy form another complex area for information systems management to deal with. The concepts of ownership of data and access to it are pivotal in trying to get a grip on this difficult area. The risk of criminal action needs to be assessed and preventive measures taken.

Securing data and systems functionality

A good start is to be clear about who owns which data and is responsible for it. This person can then be responsible for its accuracy, and can decide on precautionary and remedial actions that will be appropriate should problems threaten. Inappropriate access to systems is a major cause of problems. According to authoritative statistics from France manipulation of input is the most common source of error and fraud.

Accessibility comes in two guises, namely access to the function of a system, and access to the information contained in it. We must establish the privileges in each sense for each user. Having a user identification (ID) and password is the first step because it is the combination of these two which is the basis of securing access to a system. When the system has identified a user and checked the password it will look up the rights of access in a table. This will make clear which program menus, commands and dialogues the user can use, and which data can be read, updated, created and deleted. These two are different and security is not specified completely until they are both dealt with. Consider the case where two users are both allowed to use the bill of materials system. One might be authorized to create new parts records and the other only to read them. However, the first might only be allowed to create parts records of a certain type (from a particular supplier, say), while the second has unrestricted access.

Separating out access to the function of a system on the one hand and the information within it on the other is an important step that is sometimes not considered at all. It should be. Some data management software makes it easy to implement and some does not. Trying to implement it at the level of the application (rather than the basic software used by the application) is difficult and to be avoided in any case where security really is critical.

Securing the physical system

Physical risks to the safe operation of a computer installation include the following:

- Irregular physical access to the building (and all associated premises such as cable trunking, communications rooms, and the like).

- Unauthorized remote access to the computer system using the communications system.

- Computing resources (documentation, magnetic media) being left in insecure places.

- Fire, flooding and power failure.

- Delinquent personnel.

- Lack of adequate recovery plans.

Basic precautions

A simple way of dealing with security is to keep complete and detailed records of access and actions taken. In this way unauthorized attempts to access the system can be detected at the earliest stage.

The term for someone who abuses access to a computer system - whether with malicious intentions or not - is 'hacker': someone who is prepared to hack their way into the system. When a hacker begins to try out ID/password combinations it becomes apparent to anyone who cares to inspect the records, although when they succeed in accessing the system they will wish to amend those records.

It is astonishing to discover what obvious and predictable passwords are sometimes used. For example, in the UK the Prestel public information service had to appeal to its users to stop using the password '0000'; systems operators who are required to access to many systems, and thus have a major problem keeping up with all the passwords, tend to use longer passwords but sometimes ones which are just as obvious. Hackers will program their computers to constantly try to access a system using lists of known frequently used passwords. A system can require the user to change passwords from time to time, but most users resent this and it is not usually done.

One of the simpler actions to deal with the remote access problem is the 'ring-back' idea. A legitimate user connects with an intelligent computer to which the user gives his or her identity. The computer acknowledges, hangs up the phone and then re-dials automatically the telephone number that it has stored against that ID. It is then necessary for the remote user to be in the proper place (or at least be beside the appropriate phone). In order to secure data it is easy to encode it with quite sophisticated techniques which will deter the casual hacker.

Delinquent personnel are much more difficult to deal with. A first step is to ensure that everyone knows what they are allowed to do, what they are obliged to do and what they must not do. A lack of clarity here will lead to the situation where employees assume the right to go anywhere and do anything. Personnel management should be geared to detecting personal problems and attitudes which might tempt staff to abuse the system and attempt fraud. They might be desperate for cash or they might hold a grudge against their employer. The manager has the opportunity of checking carefully on new employee backgrounds, keeping close to employees to make sure there are no grudges lurking, and attending to routine matters such as returning card-keys which are no longer needed.

The computer 'virus' is another threat which must be dealt with. There are ways of detecting and eliminating them but it is better to be sure that they cannot get into the system in the first place. The problem is not only comparable to biological viruses because of the ways that they spread. They also evolve in a way that makes them harder and harder to detect. One important difference of course is that the computer virus is originated and evolved by human beings and not by natural processes. An organizational culture which is based on meticulous attention to detail is likely to be more secure than one which is not.

Recovery

A way of recovering from problems needs to be planned before it is needed. There will be a trade off, in the cost of alternative procedures and facilities and the probability that the problem will occur. Formal risk analysis is a way to deal with this.

Some steps which might provide easier recovery include the following:

- Acquiring alternative premises with and installing compatible equipment.
- Sharing such premises with other businesses that use the same kind of computer and operating software.
- Contracting the use of alternative facilities through one of the companies that specialize in disaster recovery centres.

- Documenting the back-up and recovery arrangements and practising them periodically to ensure that they really work.

- Ensuring that all files, applications software systems and operating software are copied periodically and placed in a safe distant location.

- Clearly allocating the responsibility for back-up and recovery with a single manager or supervisor.

Any action needs to be balanced against the cost, and might have to reflect overall corporate policy in the matter of risk management.

Project management

Although systems development projects and the approach to their management has been described in the previous chapter, the role of project management in ensuring effective use of the IS resource must not be underestimated. The proper use of project management techniques will help to avoid problems because it provides a means of detecting and resolving many of the issues earlier than would otherwise be possible. The ability of project managers to understand business as well as technical issues is an important factor in achieving success. For example, one organization sometimes uses 'follow the sun' systems development. Work is broken down into packages of less than eight hours duration each, and as one team on one continent finishes they pass it westwards - from Europe to North America, and then on to Japan, and back to Europe again. In this way projects are completed up to three times more quickly. The work is passed around on networks which allow the rapid transmittal of large volumes of data (about the project, and comprising the outputs of the project).

Formalized project management methods exist, such as 'PRINCE' - the United Kingdom government standard - which depends heavily upon prescribed project management organization and procedures. Some methods work on a total life-cycle basis - from conception to operation and phase-out. As the mix of development activity continues to become more complex the discipline which allows many projects to co-exist at the same time, at different stages but sharing the same resources, will become an important feature of information systems support. Project management is actually bigger than the individual project and some would say that *programme management* is the discipline which can handle the conflicting demands of many concurrent projects as well as the maintenance and ad hoc work that so often predominates.

Quality management

The total quality management (TQM) approach to business has been popular and the benefits are apparent, although by no means universally in all organizations which have tried it. Given the evident difficulty in delivering the information system that the user needs, at the right time and at the expected price, the vogue for quality management in information systems is understandable.

TQM is unhesitating and unremitting in its commitment to the 'zero defect' policy. Quality is built in at the start, it is argued, not tested in at the end. The purists argue that investment in testing should be withheld in favour of investing in getting it right first time. It seems that the challenge to IS management out of the total quality management culture is to build software that does not need testing.

How can this be reconciled with what we know about the actual quality of information systems? Surely we must admit that there is often a very high level of defects in the software and systems that we deliver today and that testing is essential if we are to reduce and eventually eliminate faults and bugs? This is particularly so in view of the current concern with safety critical systems. With an increasing dependence on systems in business and life at large, and with a legal obligation on suppliers to ensure that software products are fit for use, the rigorous approach to software development is both popular and has shown benefits. There are formal schemes for assessment of quality in systems development under standards such as ISO 9000 - the international standard for quality management systems, but without the commitment of management and staff there is no hope of significantly improving quality in the first place, and in maintaining it in the longer term. It takes time, and it seems to be an intolerable burden to those companies that want to move more quickly.

Consider for a moment the portfolio model presented earlier. Clearly, any oppressive quality management attitude which insists on the use of standard procedures will conflict with the needs of high potential and strategic applications. On the other hand, the need for excellence in the finished key operational system implies a rigorous repeatable approach. If we view quality management through the strategic grid we might conclude that the top half is something to do with hearts and minds, whereas the bottom half is about excellent, traditional, software engineering.

Capacity management

When computer systems are large and complex it is necessary to plan for their enhancement as demand increases. This is a well known problem but there are no simple solutions. It is similar to conventional manufacturing capacity management in many respects, for example in the identification and breaking down of workloads. It is easier to work with the analysis of smaller components that can be more readily estimated and then aggregated into an overall demand model. This is not a widely available skill and only the larger computer users would normally have a capacity management group. The capacity management group needs to have an eye on the business as well as on the technology, so that future demand is understood in business terms first (number of customers, sales orders, invoices, and so on) and then translated into technology requirements (processors, disk drives, communications lines). It needs to be able to relate business activity at the higher level to message rates and data transfers in the operational computer systems. Further, it needs to be able to extrapolate this to the supporting housekeeping activity which makes no direct contribution but assures the accuracy, resilience and recoverability of those systems.

Finally there is the question of charge-back arrangements and the way in which demand can be better managed by fine-tuning charging structures. The operation of today's real-time systems becomes increasingly elastic: the pricing structure in relation to the perceived value of the product becomes critical in keeping the user or customer happy, and in maintaining the level of service at a time when more and more businesses are considering contracting out their IT infrastructure so that others who are more expert or economical can take them over.

Summary

There are different supporting activities which are necessary to sustain a viable and effective information systems function. Together they can be seen as an infrastructure which will sustain the information systems resource at a level well above the individual project or business application.   Managing this infrastructure is a complex challenge because there is always new thinking and new methods and tools with which to achieve it.

The abstract and intangible nature of the information systems resource amplifies many of the problems normally faced in applying techniques such as quality management and capacity management. Interestingly, it is the computer which comes to our aid in trying to handle this complexity.   In the future management of the information systems resource will rely increasingly upon specialized supporting information technology.   In effect, good systems for the information systems department itself.

9

Organization for managing IS/IT

Introduction

The direct support that is provided to a project and the context within which it is enacted are one of the important factors for success. However, as described in Chapter 4 there is a need to manage applications and IS/IT generally in the preceding strategic and planning phases. This is necessary to ensure that IS/IT investments are related directly to the development of the business itself; that the investments deliver the greatest overall benefit; and that systems are implemented successfully in order to achieve those benefits. These three high-level requirements have been explained in previous chapters. In Chapter 6 generic strategies were described which provide guidance as to the best way to manage the portfolio of applications in accord with their expected business contribution.

To achieve success in practice these must be brought together into organizational structures and policies, defining how things will be managed, by whom and how the various responsibilities are related. These structures and relationships must be capable of carrying through what has been decided and be able to accommodate and interpret all the changing circumstances which will undoubtedly affect the strategy in its implementation.

The organizational approach must consider a number of key issues, including the following:

- The positioning of IT specialist resources within the organizational structure, where the bulk of the supply capability is located and to whom it reports.

- How the required people and skills are to be acquired, developed and deployed. Competent IS/IT skills are in short supply and those people's expectations have to be satisfied as well as the organization's resource needs.

- How the suppliers of technologies and services will be dealt with and the required resources procured.

- How applications and activities are co-ordinated and controlled in a multi-project, multi-user, multi-skilled environment which will cross normal organizational boundaries.

- Ensuring the creation of a culture which enables good interpersonal relationships to exist between business people and IS/IT specialists.

- How conflict and contention for resources will be resolved when they arise (as they inevitably will).

There are undoubtedly other issues. One (already referred to) is how the costs of IT are transferred to the business - traditionally called charge-out. Something which is often seen merely as an accounting or administrative issue can cause major problems if not considered carefully from the user and IS/IT management perspective. The main problem is that charge-out is actually a transfer pricing mechanism and is seen by the business managers as the price they have to pay for IT. If that pricing system is inappropriate then managers may make tactical buying decisions which are inconsistent with the strategy. Much has been written elsewhere about this subject, and it is an aspect of IS/IT management for which coherent policies need to be established and understood by all concerned. The policies should, as far as possible, be related to policies for charging-out/pricing other service functions.

Returning to the organizational issues mentioned above, it seems that wherever the main resources are located within the organization, there is a need to overlay the formal organizational relationships with a further IS/IT management structure. An IS/IT management steering group, or similar, is usually the result. Eighty per cent of major organizations in both the public and private sectors have them. If IS/IT resources are located centrally then the steering group has to ensure the resource is being used appropriately in meeting business priorities.

If resources are distributed the steering group has to ensure that applications are developed in the most coherent overall pattern, especially when they could be used across the company. In the first case the steering group is directing the IT department, and in the second it is co-ordinating the business IS/IT activities. Since there seems to be no single ideal way of organizing and locating the IS/IT resources, some such steering mechanism is probably necessary. This can then deal with questions of centralization and decentralization, and work to bridge the gap between the business and the IT department.

Centralization versus decentralization

Viewed from an organizational perspective the history of IS/IT in many organizations has been a struggle for control of resources usually between the central and peripheral parts of the business. This might have been based on geography (head office versus the regions) or function (corporate finance versus the functional departments). Obviously a number of factors will affect the advantages of either approach, for example the culture of the organization as well as its geography and management structure.

In highly centralized organizations there is a natural tendency to centralize major shared resources such as IS/IT, whereas if managers are expected to behave autonomously the reverse is true. The changing nature and economics of the technology enabled more decentralization in the 1980s, although latterly businesses have recognized that synergy and integration by means of IS/IT offer significant additional benefits and so the drive is towards centralization through IST/IT, rather than in literal terms.

Equally importantly, in the past IT specialists tended to produce systems to meet user needs and the need for co-ordinated and efficient means of production suggested that a central supply mechanism was best. Today more systems can be purchased in the form of packages, and users can easily develop some systems themselves, given a degree of technical assistance. Therefore, the IT specialists have had to develop a new orientation which is to provide a service enabling users to meet their own requirements. Often this is achieved through an information centre or an end-user support group which assists users and coordinates the procurement and dissemination of technology.

Central IT control

If a central IT group is allowed to dominate (essentially creating a monopoly) a number of problems can result:

- Forcing new systems to integrate with existing (often much older) ones and hence limiting the use of packages and an insistence on 'building' everything, resulting in very high levels of internal maintenance activity and cost.

- Insistence on 'system development methodologies' being followed in all cases, with achievement of the business benefits being secondary to achievement of the process. Users can become very frustrated.

- Decisions will be heavily technically biased and a conservative view of technology will prevail, with little innovation.

The benefit of a central IT group us that highly skilled resources can be developed and sustained, providing a clear career development path for IT specialists. The lack of dependence on key individuals will protect the investment in systems.

User control

Where user discretion dominates IS/IT decision making (free market) a different set of problems may result:

- Localized, short-term focus on problems, producing incompatible systems, which also results in a high maintenance overhead which is difficult to identify and quantify.

- Poor quality control of systems and data.

- Low levels of skill due to scattered resources - with little exchange of skills - resulting in low levels of real productivity in delivering systems, and problems in hiring and keeping good IT staff.

- Loss of effectiveness in the applications, for example poor buying leverage with suppliers due to lack of co-ordination of purchases.

On the other hand, the systems will address real current business issues on a local basis, providing the skills are available to deliver them.

Neither of these extremes includes any element of central planning, which is needed if strategic opportunities are to be identified and delivered successfully. They both effectively ignore the role which senior management can and should play in deciding what investments are made. Hence a balance must be found between centralizing and decentralizing, establishing where each is most effective and then adding the senior management role through some executive (or steering group) mechanism. This should not be too difficult to achieve within one business unit or coherent organizational entity, but it is more difficult in a multi-unit organization. The rationale explained in Chapter 6 regarding potential cross-unit benefits within the application portfolio offers some guidance, being based on the realities of the business environment rather than the politics of the organization.

The major processes and responsibilities

Figure 9.1 outlines the major processes which have to be carried out and their interrelationships based on the more detailed arguments presented earlier in this book. The structure not only indicates the major processes which need to be carried out, but also addresses the need to link direction setting, planning and implementation both to get the right things done and to provide feedback and control as discussed in Chapter 4 (see Figure 4.2).

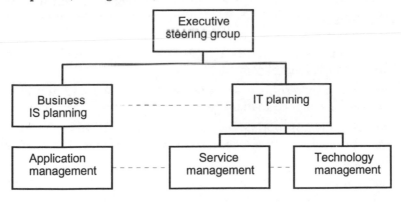

Figure 9.1   Organizational requirements

The main responsibilities of each 'box' can be considered as follows, starting at the highest, direction setting level.

Executive steering group

This is a consortium of senior managers including the most senior IT managers, with responsibility for the central planning of strategic applications and for establishing the appropriate organizational responsibilities and relationships. This involves:

- interpreting business and corporate strategy and agreeing overall IS/IT policies;
- establishing priorities, resolving contention, agreeing overall expenditure and authorizing major investments;
- setting the overall direction and monitoring business critical IS/IT projects;
- agreeing the degree of centralization/decentralization, allocating overall responsibility and establishing the right culture and attitudes to achieve co-operation and co-ordination at lower levels.

The next level is then responsible for converting the overall direction to realizable plans and providing relevant feedback on progress.

Business IS planning

This is an integral part of the business planning process for the unit or major business function, which involves the following:

- co-ordinating and prioritizing all IS activities in the business area, including agreeing budgets, approving proposals and resource allocations to particular projects;
- identifying business needs, opportunities and potential threats and assessing the IS implications;
- ensuring user resources are adequately supplied and appropriate people are assigned to manage the projects;
- ensuring the appropriate benefits are identified and achieved, and that business changes associated with systems are managed successfully.

In many cases major projects will cross business boundaries and again this layer of the structure is responsible for the co-ordination of activities across those boundaries.

IT planning

This is a line responsibility of the IT senior manager. The IT management team deals with:

- interpreting external IT trends to the benefit of the organization;
- ensuring resources are deployed to meet the business priorities;

- developing the IT resources and services in line with demand and within the policies agreed. In particular, the development of the skills and approaches to ensure projects can be achieved and productivity is improved over time;

- managing the supply of technology and specialist bought-in services to the organization;

- ensuring that technical risks are commensurate with the business benefits and risks of major investments.

The responsibilities are essentially those of supply side management, whether they control these activities directly or indirectly. To balance this the business IS planning role has to deal with demand side issues and the executive group must resolve or reconcile any demand/supply imbalances.

At the implementation level there are three major processes.

Application management

Application management is a process which must be led by user management. It is the business which has to live with the real consequences of systems investments and in the long term each part of the business will get what it deserves, depending upon the quality and quantity of the business management applied to the systems' development and operation. This applies both to major system developments where the bulk of the resource and skills are provided by the IT department, and where the system is resourced totally within the business area. Key aspects are as follows:

- identifying, specifying and quantifying the needs, benefits, resources and costs of any application to enable management to make informed evaluations and establish project priorities;

- managing projects and installed systems to ensure they meet business needs;

- ensuring business changes associated with the systems are understood and implemented, and that user resources on the system are appropriately deployed (especially where projects cross organizational boundaries);

- ensuring specialist resources are deployed to achieve the project development, and that ongoing service levels are agreed and met.

Service management

This may reside wholly within the IT function or be wholly or partly distributed to the business units (especially in large organizations). Such services include systems development, computer operations, information centres, network services, data administration, etc. The service group orientation is towards the applications to ensure the business needs are met in the most effective way. This also provides the co-ordination and experience transfer across applications, which are inevitably developed over extended periods of time and rarely ideally synchronized. Particularly important are the following:

- translating needs into technical and resource implications and developing overall skills and methods accordingly;

- monitoring performance to agreed service levels and delivery targets;

- ensuring technology is acquired and tested to minimize the risk of application failure;

- bringing appropriate (internal or external) specialist resources together to satisfy system requirements;

- planning the development of services and associated resources to intercept changing user demand.

The service groups will in some ways act as intermediaries between business people and technical specialists who so often have little in common. The people in the service groups must understand both points of view and speak the language of each to ensure effective translation from demand to supply.

Technology management

Unless the organization is a highly diversified conglomerate, managed mainly as a set of investments which are continually traded, if any aspect of IS/IT should remain centralized then it is technology management. This is the management of hardware, operating systems software, and telecommunications. All of these require highly skilled specialists if a business is to achieve the best from the technology and to deal effectively with IT suppliers. The key aspects are as follows:

- understanding technology developments, formulating options and informing others of the implications;

- assessing the capabilities of technologies against known needs;

- planning and managing the introduction of new technology (and the migration away from obsolescent technologies) to minimize the risk to existing and future business applications;
- supporting the service groups in managing the technology changes associated with changing demand;
- ensuring that technical problems can be resolved expeditiously either within the organization or in conjunction with the suppliers.

Summary of responsibilities

These lists of responsibilities are not meant to be exhaustive, but they do show the range of things that must be managed well over time and they partition those responsibilities in a balanced way between the business and the IT specialists, within a structure which will enable effective co-ordination.

Organizational issues

During the last twenty years the position (and therefore the perceived importance) of IT management has gradually risen in the organization. That is not to say the incumbent IT manager has always risen with the job, since as the role has been seen to be more important, so the managerial skills required have become greater. The best technician rarely makes the best executive but until the 1980s most IT managers had a profoundly technical background.

According to all that has been argued before, information and IS applications pervade the whole business and their management is the responsibility of every line manager. 'Demand side management' implies a collective executive responsibility. However, there are many aspects of supply side (or IT) management which need to be managed together, often centrally. Whether that department should report to the chief executive officer (CEO) or through another executive is a matter of debate and should really depend upon both how critical IT is to long-term business success and how similar service groups within the organization report into the executive structure.

In a bank, for instance, IT is the fundamental technology and an IT manager at director level would seem logical (not that an IT specialist should necessarily fill the job). In a high technology company where IT is just one of a number of technologies, the IT manager might well report to a technical director. Where IT is primarily seen as a commercial weapon critical to the future of the business, such as in retailing, IT is likely to report through a commercial or business development executive. If IT is still only (or is seen to be only) an administrative support tool then it may well report through finance or some other essentially administrative/services executive, as has often been the case in the past.

Normally as the application portfolio matures and the business dependency on IS/IT increases, so the IT manager migrates up through the hierarchy. At the same time, it becomes more probable that the person filling the job will come from the business rather than the IT department. The reverse is also true, that some organizations expect *any* future executive to have passed through an IT management position in order to be fully equipped to hold an executive post.

IS resource and the application portfolio

Whole books have been written on the subject of the title of this chapter. In this book it is only possible to provide a broad understanding of the major issues plus some insight into critical aspects of them. Getting simple, low-level things wrong can cause major business problems.

It is important not only to adopt a relevant management strategy in each segment of the application portfolio, but also to ensure that the right management skills are applied to the projects in the segment. As seen in Chapter 6 the driving forces (and hence requirements) in each segment differ and therefore need different management approaches or styles. The best laid plans can go awry if the individual responsible cannot deal with the types of issue that will arise. Equally, over time an application may well migrate round the matrix as its role in the business changes and as the strategy for its management changes; the skills which are required to manage it successfully will change. This rationale is similar to that used in managing a product portfolio.

High potential

High potential applications someone to 'champion' them through the early stages of uncertainty, or to stop the investment if no potential exists. This implies a highly self-motivated individual who (perhaps selfishly) expects recognition of personal success but equally will not wish to be associated with failure: a risk taker, not constrained by the rules and able to trigger innovation and change. Shrewd personal judgement rather than obedience to formal management processes is most valuable. However such an individual is rarely a good team leader nor especially committed to the organization's goals and would be dangerous on projects in other segments of the portfolio.

Strategic

Strategic applications require more careful nurturing to gain organizational acceptance based on a clear alignment to the business objectives. A 'developer' style of manager is required - someone who plans well, acquires and develops the necessary resources to achieve the agreed objective - seeing his or her success being dependent on demonstrating a contribution to the success of the business. An organization climber whose career in the organization is paramount, and on whose coat tails others are keen to ride, is ideal. The necessary attributes include planning, good team management and flexibility to changing circumstances, while keeping the prime objective clearly in view.

Key operational

Key operational applications need a different style: 'controller' is a good term for it. Someone who is risk averse and who requires procedure and rules to be followed in order to ensure nothing can go wrong. He or she will organize resources to maximize quality control, even if speed is sacrificed. This all helps to ensure that systems will not fail due to careless change control or lack of conformance to policy and procedure. Such a management style thrives in relatively stable situations and can produce stability out of turbulence by strict adherence to the rules. Clearly an entrepreneur and a controller are quite different - even opposite - characters.

Support

Support applications require a 'caretaker' approach: someone who gets satisfaction from achieving the impossible with no resources at all, but who likes to have that ability recognized. It is a reactive, problem solving approach. Getting each job done expediently and to the satisfaction of the user is more important than long-term planning. The corporate goals do not figure highly on this manager's priorities, but ensuring small problems do not become major corporate nightmares, and hence solving them adeptly, does.

Consequences of getting it wrong

The skills of each type of manager are relevant to the different segments of the portfolio and each is equally valuable. We can also see the dangers of getting the wrong type of manager into the wrong segment. Forced into unfamiliar and alien territory, anyone is likely to fail and now we begin to see the reasons why. Getting the right people is just as important as getting the right strategy. In a similar way, the way in which the IT specialists are deployed across the application portfolio will determine the long-term capability of the organization to deliver successful systems.

Internal and external sourcing of the IS resource

External sourcing

Bringing in outside resources has a number of potential benefits. It can reduce the burden on internal resources, spread risk, provide access to specialist skills, and reduce the overall cost of the outsourced operations. Of course, there are dangers. Consider the following increasingly common scenario:

> *The existing IT professionals are bogged down in the maintenance of a whole range of old key operational and support systems. A new major strategic application is conceived and the internal staff cannot be released in the timescale required. The decision is taken to bring in an external organization to develop the system.*

The following are some of the consequences:

1. The contractor may have been given an open ended contract to meet the ever changing needs of the strategic system - almost a blank cheque.

2. No one in the IT department is capable of understanding and eventually taking responsibility for maintaining the system, nor is there any real motivation to do so.

3. The contractor has gained some very useful knowledge which might be resold to a competitor.

4. Demoralized internal staff who have been left doing the boring old work, which does not enhance their skills, often leave and in some cases join the contractor.

Thus, outsourcing can become a vicious circle, but one which can be avoided if the organization's own staff are employed on the more important strategic systems and outside resources are confined to key operational and support systems. The outsourced resource could further be confined to delivery and maintenance of the system, especially where packages can be employed.

Setting the boundary and finding a balanced approach

The boundary of what is being outsourced is clearly a critical issue and it does not have to embrace everything. In the short term limited outsourcing may appear unattractive, but in the long term it develops the abilities of the organization and will enable good staff to be attracted and kept. Bearing in mind the continuing shortage of skilled IT professionals this is a key aspect of IS/IT management.

In striving to achieve the right balance of internal and external resourcing and to understand the relationship with the rest of the business, we need to understand the differences between at least four options (see Figure 9.2):

- *An intimate relationship* between IT and business where the use of external resources would be minimized. The closeness of the relationship is the source of real business advantage.

- *An organizational relationship* where the IT department is seen to add value, but not within an intimate relationship. Here we see the beginnings of potentially useful outsourcing, especially for non-competitive key operational systems development and operation.

- *A contractual relationship* where the IT department is seen as a cost, which could probably be reduced by wide scale outsourcing to the cheapest bidder. This is appropriate where there is no competitive advantage, just the need for a competent professional service.

- *A strictly financial relationship* where cost is the only determinant, and where we have sometimes turned the IT department into a profit centre to 'prove' that value exceeds cost (or otherwise!). This situation arises most often when the finance department has been responsible for IS and IT.

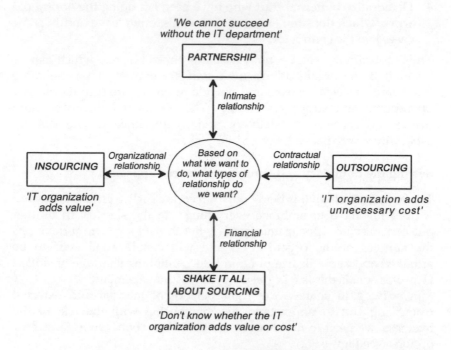

Figure 9.2   IS sourcing in a 'mixed economy'

More than one of these approaches may apply in the case of a 'mixed economy' but at best most organizations only consider three, depending on how they view IT. The poor record of IT in delivering business benefit is the usual reason for choosing to outsource, leading to a strictly contractual relationship with defined service and performance levels. This can work well when the organization has a cultural bias to the use of outside contractors, as in the case of the construction industry. In other sectors, where the core business is more information intensive, the organizational ability to manage information and deliver strategically effective systems is critical to future success, and here outsourcing would not be a good idea.

Business strategies are increasingly based on the idea of the *competencies* which the business can deploy. This attitude allows a more open approach to product and marketplace. Consider, for example, the financial services sector, where the competency to manage funds (and to address customer needs), has led to a blurring of the traditional boundaries between banks, loan organizations, and insurance companies. Here the ability to deploy information and information systems for competitive advantage is critical to success, and the partnership approach is the most appropriate for the core business applications. Sadly, there is still too often a cultural gap between the attitude of the IT people and the business at large, which jeopardizes the chances of success.

Bridging the culture gap

IS/IT is a relatively new and immature management discipline. Technology continues to evolve rapidly and the management issues continue to change. This has demanded the development of new specialists, mostly young, who see their career in IT as the primary objective and their employer as secondary. Given the ever increasing demand for their skills they are very mobile. Consequently this situation can develop a major culture gap between the values of the business managers and the personal ambitions and values of the IT specialists in the organization. Meeting business needs is less important to the IT specialists than developing marketable skills. Into this yawning chasm of misunderstanding and mistrust have fallen many potentially important investments, having failed to deliver any benefits and having incurred inordinate costs.

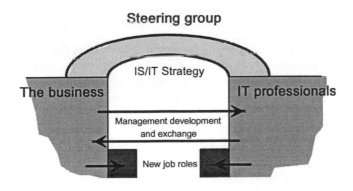

Figure 9.3 Bridging the culture gap

Somehow the gap must be bridged, while allowing for and respecting the particular needs of the people involved in a fast developing and increasingly critical business function. A number of things can be done to achieve this balance between integrating the IT function more effectively with the mainstream of the business and accommodating its special issues. Figure 9.3 depicts some of the key things which organizations are doing to reduce the gulf of misunderstanding that will otherwise inhibit real progress.

At the highest level the steering group provides a forum for discussing IS/IT in the business context. Developing a coherent IS/IT strategy provides a common sense of direction and commitment to a set of agreed goals and an understanding of the value IS/IT has in the business. Building IT management positions into the general management development programme, ensuring specialists can gain business management experience (and vice versa) reduces the fear of the unknown and improves the overall management competence of both. At a lower level still, the development of new job roles - such as information specialists in business functions and IT specialists dedicated to providing services to a business client area - provide the means by which understanding continually develops.

Many organizations are trying all these ideas simultaneously in order to bridge the gap. Without at least some constructive measures being taken, nothing will change and the future will produce even more disappointment than in the past. Which organization can afford that, in today's difficult and dynamic business environment?

Summary

Not only has the IS resource to be managed to meet the requirements of today, it must be developed to meet the needs of the future. Part of the challenge is to ensure that technical aspects of IS/IT are well managed and that appropriate supporting disciplines and capabilities are in place. We need also an understanding of the long-term issues.

Expediency today often leads to problems and poor productivity over the long term. Another part of the resource management problem is bringing the total resource into alignment with the mainstream of the business, and hence fitting it appropriately into the processes of the organization. As in many aspects of business, the people are ultimately the real resource, and when specialists are scarce their needs must be accommodated and their skills must be deployed effectively.

Because the use and management of technology is becoming better understood, it is being used in a greater variety of ways, to do increasingly complex tasks. At the same time, competitive environments are becoming more intense and businesses are becoming more dependent on IS/IT for success. Relevant IS/IT skills are scarce and will become scarcer. Effective IS/IT resource management will become more important, not less so.

10

Conclusion: current and future directions

This book has presented a view of information systems which deals with management issues according to different viewpoints: the viewpoint of the business which needs the benefit of new information systems, and that of the IT professionals who need to understand how best to serve the business. It has introduced a number of different tools which help managers to get to grips with the process of analyzing strategic needs, organizing the resource and undertaking systems development projects.

At the heart of this book is the applications portfolio model which separates out the different kinds of need, the benefits available and the different approaches to systems building and delivery. Because it separates out the different applications it helps us to summarize the situation in businesses today.

Most organizations have many applications in the lower half of the portfolio model. This is because they are the easiest to justify financially, and financial justification is a prerequisite in most organizations. The trend is for organizations to seek new applications in the upper half of the portfolio, thereby taking advantage of the future potential that information systems offer as well as the current advantage. There needs to be a process within every organization that makes this possible: for individual users to follow through an intuitive thought about what IT could do for them, for business units to analyze more carefully their competitive situation, and for the organization at large to take advantage of industry-level initiatives which are at the leading edge of current thinking.

At the start of this book is a model for the evolution of information systems (see Figure 2.4). In the light of current and future developments we can re-evaluate that model to show how ideas are changing and how the scope of our purpose and vision is extending. Figure 10.1 takes the original model an develops it. With this extended model we can position business process redesign as the means by which we achieve internal integration and business network redesign as the means by which we achieve external integration. We can also see a fourth stage in the evolution of information systems, which is about enhancing relationships and which is focused at the organizational level.

Primary purpose - - >

	Efficiency	Effectiveness	Underpin integration	Enhance relationships
Internal	Traditional data processing for support systems	Key operational and managagement information systems	Internal integration (business process redesign)	Global inter-business unit activity
External	Electronic Data Interchange	Information sharing	External integration (business network redesign)	Supplier customer relationships
	Task	Function	Process	Organisations

Primary focus - ->

Figure 10.1   The further evolution of information systems

This reminds us that the limits to what we can achieve are not technological, they are human. It is our ability to conceptualize and communicate ideas - especially across organizational boundaries - which currently limits our ability to deploy information technology and all that goes with it. In essence, as this book explains, it is the *information system* that provides the benefit - the information technology just provides yet another cost.

The future for the IT department

As users learn that they too can effect change through the championing of information systems and systems-based ideas, the message for the IT professional is that the future will be very different. Businesses will know much more clearly what they want, and they will need less help in managing IS developments. The IT department will fall back to the provision of infrastructure and support for operational systems.

Infrastructure includes the hardware and networks that are needed to support the operation of systems - far more diffuse today that it used to be. The old model of the 'mainframe computer in the basement' is being challenged and distributed hardware is seen as the platform for the next generation of systems. Compatibility with the infrastructure of business partners becomes an issue that IT people have to deal with as systems become more integrated. We are still at an early stage in understanding how to manage distributed systems, however, and the resilience of these systems does not match the reliability of the mainframe. Organizations which operate both kinds of platform report that the cost of supporting networks of personal computers and workstations can be five times higher than the cost of the mainframe and there are already some famous cases where multi-million pound projects have been cancelled with no benefit other than simple experience. The learning curve for any major new technology is at least ten years and we have learnt to be sceptical about recurring technological hype.

The future for the business community

Since the first signs of electronic data interchange in the early 1980s, our ability to develop inter-organizational systems and industry-level systems has been developing. Running a business is going to become ever more dependent upon systems links with other businesses.

There are now standard electronic messages which minimize the investment in converting paper document exchange into electronic data exchange. Industries have agreed coding schemes for products and location references, and this standardization is leading to wide scale adoption of 'electronic' co-operation.

For example. the United States Department of Defense is investing massively in fully integrated systems that fundamentally change the way that defence procurement and logistics is organized among the involved parties, and the high-technology business that are close to this market are getting the message. Advanced thinking about integrated systems is spilling over into all aspects of the aerospace industry, and is being picked up and tested by other sectors such as the UK process engineering industry.

One result of this DoD initiative is the ability to specify, fully electronically, every aspect of a product: its design, its composition, the properties of the materials from which it is made, and the processes by which it is made. The ability to instantly transmit *all* the information that a factory (and its logistics support system) needs to begin production of new product is just over the next horizon.

The future for management

Above all else, this book has taken a management perspective. There has been much written about the future for management and this is not the place to try to restate what has been better said elsewhere.

However, in the matter of information systems management now has the ability to harness and control the investment in IS/IT, and to focus it in a direction that best matches their ambitions for their business. Our ability to manage IS/IT more effectively with the right tools and techniques will lead to more rapid and extensive deployment of systems. So much is obvious.

What is less obvious is the effect that information systems will have on the management process itself. Systems thinking has come from our long years of experience with information systems, and it can change the way that managers think. In history we have built businesses on craft skills, hierarchical management systems or simple financial clout. Now is the time to consider how new forms and structures for business can be devised, which will be based on our ability to 'think systems' and to deploy information as the primary business asset.

Index